Dan Rice, DVM

Chesapeake Bay Retrievers

**Everything About Purchase,
Care, Nutrition, Behavior,
and Training**

**With 44 Photographs
Illustrations by Tana Hakanson**

BARRON'S

About the Author

Dan Rice, a veterinarian from Colorado, is presently pursuing a lifelong writing avocation. A professional member of Dog Writers Association of America, he has written an anthology of veterinary practice experiences and is now busily composing children's stories. *Chesapeake Bay Retrievers* is the eighth pet book he has written for Barron's; others include *Bengal Cats, The Complete Book of Dog Breeding, The Complete Book of Cat Breeding, Akitas, Dogs from A to Z: A Dictionary of Canine Terms, The Well-Mannered Cat,* and *Brittanys.* Now retired in Arizona with his wife Marilyn, he keeps in touch with canine research and the fancy through study and writing.

Dedication

This book is dedicated to two exceptional individuals, Tim and Ethel.

All inquiries should be addressed to:
Barron's Educational Series, Inc.
250 Wireless Boulevard
Hauppauge, NY 11788
http://www.barronseduc.com

International Standard Book No. 0-7641-0657-0

Library of Congress Catalog Card No. 98-29267

Library of Congress Cataloging-in-Publication Data
Rice, Dan, 1933–
    Chesapeake Bay retrievers : everything about purchase, care, nutrition, behavior, and breeding / Dan Rice. illustrations by Tana Hakanson.
        p. cm.—(A complete pet owner's manual)
    Includes bibliographical references (p. 99) and index.
    ISBN 0-7641-0657-0
    1. Chesapeake Bay retrievers. I. Title. II. Series.
SF429.C4R535   1999
636.752'7—dc21   98–29267
                                         CIP

Printed in Hong Kong

987654321

Photo Credits

Donna J. Coss: pages 25, 37, 64, 93; Kent and Donna Dannen: pages 4, 17, 45, 53, 89; Tara Darling: pages 16, 57, 65, 80; Isabelle Francise: pages 28, 29 bottom, 41, 52; Bruce and Jeane Harkins: page 96; Zig Leszczynski: page 8; Dan F. Rice: pages 20, 61, 88; Joanne and Stanley H. Silver: page 29 top; Judith E. Strom: pages 24, 32, 36, 48, 68, 69, 72 top and bottom, 81 bottom, 84, 97; Toni Tucker: pages 12, 13, 56, 81 top, 100, 101.

Cover Photos

Perry Phillips: Front cover—American, Canadian, Puerto Rico, and World Champion Silvercreeks I Love Lucy, CGC/TDI, DELTA; Kent and Donna Dannen: inside front cover; Toni Tucker: inside back cover and back cover.

Important Note

This pet owner's guide tells the reader how to buy and care for a Chesapeake Bay Retriever. The author and the publisher consider it important to point out that the advice given in the book is meant primarily for normally developed puppies from a good breeder—that is, dogs of excellent physical health and good temperament.

Anyone who adopts a fully grown dog should be aware that the animal has already formed its basic impressions of human beings. The new owner should watch the animal carefully, including its behavior toward humans, and should meet the previous owner. If the dog comes from a shelter, it may be possible to get some information on the dog's background and peculiarities there. There are dogs that, as a result of bad experiences with humans, behave in an unnatural manner or may even bite. Only people that have experience with dogs should take in such animals.

Caution is further advised in the association of children with dogs, in meeting with other dogs, and in exercising the dog without a leash.

Even well-behaved and carefully supervised dogs sometimes do damage to someone else's property or cause accidents. It is therefore in the owner's interest to be adequately insured against such eventualities, and we strongly urge all dog owners to purchase a liability policy that covers their dog.

Contents

Preface 5

Introduction 6
Origin of the Domestic Dog 6
Human Influence 7
Specialization 8
Chessie History 8

Appreciating Your Chesapeake 14
The Chesapeake's Swimming
 Ability 14
Dual-Purpose Dog? 17
Think Before You Buy 20

Selecting Your Chessie 21
Are You Ready for a Dog? 21
Is a Chessie the Right Dog? 22
Choosing the Right Chessie 23
Type of Chessie 25
HOW-TO: Perform an On-the-Spot
 Health Inspection 26
Finding the Right Breeder 28
Health Records 30

**Taking Your Chesapeake Puppy
 Home 31**
First Days in Your Home 31
A Chessie Puppy in Your
 Yard 35
Exercise 36
Chewing 37
Automobiles 37
Boarding Kennels 38
Veterinary Care 38
Identification 39

Training Your Chesapeake 40
Housebreaking 40
Collar and Leash Training 42
Elementary Obedience
 Training 43

Feeding Your Chesapeake 50
Types of Foods 50
Varieties of Dry Food 51
Dog Food Labels 52
Nutritional Elements 53
Frequency of Feeding 55
Dietary No-No's 55
Inappropriate Eating Habits 55

Grooming Your Chessie 57
When to Groom 57
HOW-TO: Groom Your
 Chesapeake 58
Calluses 60
Teeth 60

Work for Your Chesapeake 62
The Versatile Chesapeake 62
Hunting and Retrieving 62
Retriever Field Trials 66
Obedience Trials 67
Tracking Dog 69
Agility Trials 70
Canine Good Citizen Certificate 71

Health Care 73
Choosing a Good Veterinarian 73
Emergencies 74

Chesapeakes are at home with decoys or the real thing.

Evaluate First 74
Other Emergencies or
    Illnesses 75
HOW-TO: Treat Emergencies 76
Preventive Medicine 78
Other Common Diseases 80
Intestinal Parasites 81
Heartworms 82
External Parasites 83
Hereditary Conditions 85
Diseases of the Aging
    Chessie 87
Euthanasia 88

Breeding Your Chessie 89
Reasons for Breeding 89
Breeding Stock Selection 90
Finding Good Homes for Pups 91

**Registering and Showing Your
    Chesapeake 92**
The American Kennel Club 92
Conformation Shows 93

Useful Addresses and Literature 99

Index 102

Preface

When John Schmidt, D.V.M. gave the Champion, professionally trained Chesapeake bitch to my son Tim, I was only mildly impressed. I knew quite a number of Chessies in John's breeding kennel, had seen a few in the training kennel that I worked with, and cared for many more as pets. I found them to be intelligent, tough, independent patients that seemed to prefer swimming to walking.

Chessies were easy to handle, but I got the impression that they only tolerated me. Unlike the Labradors and Goldens that galloped into my exam room, licked my face, and left muddy footprints all over my shoes and pants, the stoic Chessie rarely displayed open emotion.

Ethel was more than two years old when she came to us, but she bonded instantly to Tim. When he wasn't home, she adopted and followed my wife about, with her sad Chesapeake eyes pleading for a quick scratch behind the ears. Peddlers avoided our home due to Ethel's surly bearing and defensive attitude, although she didn't actually bite anyone.

All her life, this fine bitch displayed great reserve and dignity. Forever aloof, she would only frisk about when playing with Tim or when one of us unlimbered a shotgun. In the field, she was all business. She would retrieve for anyone, but always took the bird or dummy to Tim.

I remember with a shiver the many early frosty mornings that were spent jump shooting ducks as they rose from the warm spring eddy ponds on the Roaring Fork River. This wonderfully willing Chesapeake was always ready to hit the water, paying little heed to the ice on the river.

She enjoyed the luxury of copious canals, rivers, and creeks to occupy her time and provide exercise between duck and pheasant seasons. She lived a long, active life in spite of hip dysplasia, the disease that ultimately precipitated her demise. She was responsible for untold hours of enjoyment for my sons and me, and her fantastic retrieving feats live on in our memories.

Acknowledgments

The late John Schmidt, D.V.M., a close personal friend and colleague for many years, added more to this book than he could have realized. In 1969, John's Snocre Kennel began breeding and promoting Chesapeakes of the finest order. His appreciation of the breed rubbed off on many of his friends and associates.

Numerous Chesapeake breeders such as Joanne Silver, Yvette Yoho, Jon and Carol Andersen, Patsy Barber, and others contributed valuable information that is included in this book. As always, my thanks to Barron's editors Mary Falcon and Sally Strauss for their advice and guidance and to evaluator Joe Stahlkuppe for his suggestions and comments.

Introduction

Origin of the Domestic Dog

Dog fanciers often wonder about the origin of *Canis familiaris*, the domestic dog. They question how present-day dogs of such a great variety of sizes and shapes can possibly share a single progenitor. They ask if retrievers and gazehounds share common ancestry with toy breeds and giant breeds. To a logical person, that seems highly unlikely at first glance. Upon closer inspection, however, regardless of their size or conformation, all dogs have certain characteristics that aren't much different from those of their wild cousins. The Canidae family to which the dog belongs includes wolves, foxes, jackals, and other species that are all somewhat similar to the domestic dog.

Recent technological information indicates that according to mitochondrial (intracellular) DNA analysis, the wolf is the progenitor of the domestic dog, or wolves and dogs had a common ancestor. The DNA report is slightly more believable when one recognizes the various sizes and colors of wolves. Those of the Northern Hemisphere are generally larger than the wolves that are seen in the southern countries. Smaller races of wolves are also indigenous to India and China.

Whether or not one concedes that dogs are actually descendants of wolves, their similarities are greater than their differences. Their teeth are adapted to seizing, slicing, and tearing. Their senses of smell and hearing are extremely well developed. Domestic dogs, like their wolf forefathers, are pack oriented; they follow the guidance of the alpha dog, or dominant member of their pack. Feral dogs, like wolves, maintain central headquarters, regions, or dens that they defend.

Dogs, like their wild cousins, use sophisticated reasoning powers to solve problems. Wild dogs hold a portion of their hunting pack in reserve to wait until the prey has been fatigued by the chase. Then a few fresh dogs jump into the fray to rush the quarry and make the kill. Bird dogs use their memories and reasoning ability to solve retrieving problems. They have learned that wounded birds must be retrieved first, and they circle in the field to cross the scent of a downed bird. Dogs have been known to prove their loyalty by pulling a drowning child from a swimming pool, or warn their sleeping

The first domesticated canines were probably wolves that followed hunters to scavenge from the game they killed.

masters of a fire. These examples hardly scratch the surface of the many stories about the thought processes and reasoning ability of the canine.

Human Influence

Ancient canines lived in packs that were much like prehistoric human communities and they probably vied with humans for an equal place in the food chain. They had many of the same predators and prey. Dogs shared a desire for warm, easily defendable dens, and even had a diet similar to that of man. It seems these two species were destined to become companions and hunting partners, joining their intelligence and adaptability to serve each other. Humans and canines have established a mutually beneficial relationship that predates written history. Their symbiotic association is abundantly recorded in petroglyphs that decorate the walls of prehistoric human homes, and it is confirmed by prominent paintings and sculptures of dogs that have been found among relics of ancient civilizations.

Domestication

Dogs were probably the first animal species to be domesticated by humans. How did the first dog form an alliance with humans? This is a provocative question. It is logical to assume that prehistoric dogs first existed apart from man. They were wolf-like carnivores that survived by hunting, killing, and eating their prey. They may have followed the cave dweller, to scavenge from the offal of the quarry that he managed to kill. Prehistoric humans were also predators, possessing a larger brain, abstract reasoning capability, and an opposable thumb, and they no doubt recognized this four-legged animal's speed and endurance.

In guessing that dogs would make useful additions to their family, cave

Specialized functions have led to the development of various breeds of dogs.

dwellers allowed puppies to join their company. Dogs that were adopted had to recognize a human as the dominant, or alpha, member of this group in order to enjoy the benefits of living with humans. These early dog breeders must have recognized a certain dog's hunting and trailing aptitude and made use of that knowledge. Prehistoric dog trainers were probably in popular demand. With canine help, other species of animals could be herded, captured, and either killed for food or domesticated.

Because they shared human domiciles and food, dogs would naturally guard those within from the intrusion of other species and other humans. Eventually, various sizes and types of dogs were purposefully bred to serve a particular need of the human, which varied tremendously from one environment to another.

Dogs that refused to submit to human domination and accept a subservient role in the community were eliminated. They were rejected from man's society, and provided meat for stew pots and pelts for human clothing. By this primitive but practical

Where do you want the firewood?

Greyhound have the speed and endurance to course wolves, elks, hares, or other game. Scenthounds like the Coonhounds and Bloodhounds have the necessary olfactory (smelling) abilities to follow a scent trail for miles. Mastiffs were originally bred to guard and defend property; the Pug was developed as a lapdog; and in some primitive societies, dogs are still raised for their meat and pelts.

Sporting breeds such as the Chesapeake Bay Retriever were originally bred with the specialized functions necessary to locate and retrieve ducks, geese, and other edible birds. They originated at a time when shooting and trapping wildlife were the principal means of feeding families and stocking larders with meat. These bird dogs were bred to minimize the number of wounded birds that escaped hunters' bags; they decreased the number of shots that must be taken to feed the family.

selection, the surviving dogs became helpmates to the people who fed, housed, and kept them.

Dogs have served humans in many roles. It is only natural that the dominant humans should select and propagate the type of dog that pleases them, the dog that can do what needs to be done. Thus, by selective breeding, there are now hundreds of different sizes, abilities, and temperaments from which to choose. Dogs became valuable and loyal accomplices in virtually every human endeavor and they rapidly earned the title "man's best friend."

Specialization

Great Danes were originally selected for their size and strength to hunt bear, boar, and other big game. Siberian Huskies and Alaskan Malamutes have developed protective coats to withstand bitter winters and the strength and stamina to pull loaded sleds through deep snow. Gazehounds such as the Saluki and

Chessie History

Quoting from B. Waters's book *Fetch and Carry, A Treatise on Retrieving,* written in 1895: "The Chesapeake Bay dog is remarkably intelligent and physically of extraordinary bone and muscle, and they are said to be indefatigable in work, and persistent in fetching to bag the most difficult birds.

"But no breed has been more neglected. Save the energetic efforts of a few breeders, nothing has been done for its public advancement. There is no dog of equal interest which has so little literature devoted to it, though none have so sensational an origin, nor have any others a field of practical usefulness wherein abounds so much interesting incident from which to make good history."

Chesapeake Bay

Chesapeake is an Indian name that is roughly translated from che-sep-ack, meaning "country on a great river." Captain John Smith so named that body of water when he explored the bay in 1608. Chesapeake Bay is a part of the Intracoastal Waterway that leads from the Atlantic Ocean northward, dividing both Virginia and Maryland. It eventually continues to Wilmington, Delaware via the Chesapeake and Delaware Canal, which connects the Delaware and Elk Rivers. The Susquehanna River of Pennsylvania marks its northern reaches.

This bay is about 195 miles long, from 3 to 25 miles wide, and is sufficiently deep for oceangoing vessels to traverse. It is the largest inlet on the Atlantic coast, and holds title to many important events in early American history (apart from being the place of origin of the Chesapeake Bay Retriever). The bay is lined with major seaports, and Norfolk Naval Base is found near its mouth. Jamestown colonists founded the first permanent English settlement in Virginia, on the shores of Chesapeake Bay in 1607. The decisive battle of the American Revolution was fought at Yorktown, on the banks of Chesapeake Bay in 1781. In the War of 1812, the British used Chesapeake Bay as an invasion route to burn the White House. It was during the British bombardment of Fort McHenry in Baltimore Harbor in 1814 that Francis Scott Key, looking out over Chesapeake Bay, penned our national anthem.

An All-American Dog

From that historical all-American location came the Chesapeake Bay Retriever, an all-American dog. This powerful bird dog rose from a game-laden, cold and turbulent body of water early in the nineteenth century. The breed was developed specifically for retrieving ducks and other waterfowl from the bay, and the Chessie excelled in that vocation. There are

The Newfoundland was the principal progenitor of the Chesapeake Bay Retriever.

several stories about the origin of the Chessie that are worthy of note. These may be true, partly true, or only colorful anecdotes.

Newfoundland Ancestry

To look at the Newfoundland breed of today, one can hardly believe that it played an intimate role in the development of the Chessie. Newfoundlands came from the area of St. John's, Newfoundland, where two varieties of Newfies were recognized. The "Lesser Newfoundland" had a shorter coat than the other. This Lesser Newfoundland is believed to be the progenitor of the Labrador Retriever as well as the Chesapeake Bay Retriever.

Most of the tales of the Chessie's parentage start out similarly. There is general agreement that there was an English brig en route to Poole Harbor, England from Newfoundland with a cargo of codfish. The ship was about to pick up a partial load of lumber from the Chesapeake Bay area when it foundered off the coast of Maryland in 1807.

The crew of the brig was saved from the wreckage, together with two puppies that were of Newfoundland lineage, but from different bloodlines. One of these puppies was a dingy red-colored male called Sailor. The other was a black bitch called Canton, the name of the salvage ship that rescued

Breaking through ice with its chest, the Chessie is an aggressive and powerful swimmer.

the brig's crew. According to reports, these puppies had coats that were short but very thick, and they both proved to be outstanding waterfowl retrievers. It is further reported that Canton lived on the Western Shore and Sailor on the Eastern Shore of Chesapeake Bay. There is no recorded mating of these two dogs, but a few researchers assume that they were so mated. These two dogs are credited with beginning the Chesapeake breed. At this point, tales diverge.

One story has it that the dogs were crossed with yellow and tan Coonhounds. That cross is said to give the Chessie its great sense of smell, yellow eyes, dead-grass color, and stamina. This account also confirms the Newfoundland blood in the original stock, which is the source of the breed's fantastic swimming ability. Also from the Newfie came a good

temper and faithfulness, as well as its thick coat.

Another version claims that Canton and Sailor were crossed with English Water Poodles. Although not usually considered a probability, that cross would account for the Chessie's oily, waterproof coat. That story is credited to O. D. Foulks who wrote about his dogs shortly after the Civil War. His dogs were called "Brown Winchesters," or "Red Chesters," which may have been a separate breed that has become extinct, or they may have been early Chesapeake Bay Retrievers. Foulks wrote that his dogs were a cross between the English Water Poodle and the Newfoundland. He describes these dogs similarly to the Chesapeake, and commented that the breed was the only real Ducking Dog that was bred and raised for that purpose.

Occasionally you might read that the Chesapeake is a descendant of "St. John's dogs," meaning those Newfies that originated in St. John's, Newfoundland. Margaret Chern, in her book *The Complete Newfoundland,* indicates that Sailor and Canton may have been bred to Water Spaniels as well.

Another reference, the *American Shooting Manual*, circa 1827, refers to the new breed as the Newfoundland Duck Dog. They have also been called the Chesapeake Bay Ducking Dog.

The American Kennel Club's *The Complete Dog Book* takes up the story of Canton and Sailor with ". . . nondescript dogs then used for retrieving were bred to them . . ." indicating that outcrosses of various other breeds and crossbreds may figure into the origin of the Chessie. That same reference indicates that the English Otterhound might have been one of those breeds, as well as the Flat-Coated and Curly-Coated Retrievers.

In the mid-1800s, Chesapeake Bay's Eastern Shore farmers and sportsmen were surely instrumental in developing the breed. Even at that time, the dog fancy attracted the attention of prosperous farmers. Later, the Chessie was adapted to the needs of the working watermen who collected oysters, fish, and waterfowl for the commercial marketplace.

Chesapeake Bay Gunners

The Eastern Shore waterman was not wealthy; he and his dog were loners. He may have worked on oyster dredges seasonally to supplement his scanty income. He lived in a shack on one of the bays or marshes, and his dog slept outside the door. This was a man who owned a boat, fishing gear, guns, and, his most valuable asset, a fine, trustworthy retriever. He survived by braving the cold and rough waters of Chesapeake Bay in a flat-bottomed skiff, shooting waterfowl and netting fish for the marketplace. It is likely that the tough Chesapeake Bay Retriever fought beside his owner when necessary to protect his meager belongings. The early Chessie's society was limited to this single individual, and the dog rarely socialized with other dogs or people.

Unlike farmers and sportsmen, the watermen weren't husbandmen; they didn't breed animals, nor is it likely that they studied the pedigrees of their dogs when they found it necessary to breed them. Their duck retrievers were judged by what they could and would do; they were evaluated by their aptitude, not by their lineage. These men delighted in the all-business, workaholic attitudes of the dogs they developed.

Historical accounts of waterfowl shooting on Chesapeake Bay in the mid-1800s indicate that the watermen sometimes used gigantic skiff-mounted shotguns to blast enormous numbers of ducks and geese from the water. Their retrievers then worked into the night to bring the hundreds of birds into the watermen's boats and blinds. Keep in mind that during this era, the principal source of fresh meat was from commercial gunners who harvested game any way they could. James Michener's novel *Chesapeake* relates a fascinating story of this technique.

Sportsmen's Interest

It wasn't until about the end of the nineteenth century that duck hunting and other outdoor sports became popular in the United States. As sportsmen learned about the rugged Chesapeake Bay Retriever, the breed became more popular and was occasionally seen on lakes and rivers from coast to coast. The Chessie flourished on the Atlantic Seaboard and was also well known in Minnesota and Manitoba. The tough and hardy Chessie was in its element wherever heavy water, adverse climate, and sub-zero weather prevailed.

It is generally agreed that the Chessie is a "one-man retriever," and the dog has also been accused of being hardheaded, difficult to train, and socially unreliable. Many Chessies won't work for anyone except their owner or handler, and those that will often do so with little enthusiasm. The typical Chesapeake will retrieve for others in the blind, as long as its handler is also present, and it is to its handler that the retrieved bird is presented.

The Chesapeake is a rough, tough individual with the courage of a lion. It loves its work and where choppy waters, strong currents, or floating ice discourage other breeds, the Chesapeake goes on about its business and brings its owners the ducks that they shoot.

In the past, the dog often weighed a hundred pounds or more, and hunters could depend on it to face all obstacles. Where the rushes are heavy, it has the weight and power to

Chessies make excellent pets as well as hunting dogs.

crash through them. When called upon to bring in a crippled Canada goose, it doesn't have to maneuver the bird to grasp it by a broken wing and then tow the bird to shore. It is big enough to get a body hold, and when the Chessie reaches the bank, it walks out with its head in the air and hands up 10 or 12 pounds of struggling goose. Regardless of where you read of the Chessie, each story tends to extol the virtues of the animal as a water retriever.

Early Appearance and Acceptance

By 1884, this courageous, tough, intelligent American dog retrieved ducks endlessly from the frigid waters of the Northeast. Soon the breed was touted by many sportsmen as "best duck dog of the Northeast," and was sufficiently uniform to be registered. The American Kennel Club source book shows that in 1887, two Chesapeakes were registered.

The American Chesapeake Club (ACC) was founded in 1918 under the leadership of Earl Henry of Albert Lea, Minnesota. The ACC was among the early sponsoring clubs of the breed that was known as the Chesapeake Bay dog. The club soon fell on hard times, but was revived in 1935 under the presidency of Anthony Bliss. He actively promoted the dog, and produced the first Dual Champion Chesapeake (Champion of Record in conformation shows and Field Champion in field trials).

In 1929, the first breed standard was established for the Chessie. This standard was similar to that of today, but differed in that the head was described as being more of a wedge shape. The first Chesapeakes were found only in dark brown colors with shading to a reddish sage, and their coats were longer and thicker than those of today. That first standard includes the following note:

"Chesapeake Bay dogs are widely known for their ability in retrieving ducks. Water is their particular element, but they are painstaking and diligent workers when retrieving any kind of game, on land or water. They are essentially an American dog."

The Chessie has not been an outstanding field trial competitor. Perhaps the average trial doesn't offer the big dog sufficient challenge. This is a breed that is less popular than other retrievers, and that may be a factor. They are courageous to a fault, and

Let's go hunting!

sometimes don't kennel well with other dogs. Professional handlers often would rather take into competitions dogs that are more tractable and docile than the rugged Chessie.

Appreciating Your Chesapeake

The Chesapeake's Swimming Ability

To watch a Chessie challenge nature's elements is an experience that you aren't likely to forget. Chessies have an overwhelming love of water, and when they enter a river or lake, they do so exuberantly, leaping out, far from the shore. It isn't uncommon to see a Chesapeake jump into a partially frozen lake, breaking through inch-thick ice with its battering-ram chest to retrieve a wounded duck. The Chessie is an accomplished swimmer that is absolutely fearless in the water. This dog may decide to take a swim in any weather, in any body of water, diving and playing, just for the exhilaration and fun of the sport. When a Chessie emerges from freezing water, a couple of good

Chessies have been reported to retrieve ducks from frozen rivers under hazardous swimming conditions.

shakes and nearly all traces of ice and moisture are gone from its oily coat.

Chesapeakes have been reported to retrieve from the Missouri River in the spring when the ice was breaking up and the river was filled with large cakes of floating ice. This durable dog would climb up on an ice cake, cross it, and plunge into the water on the far side, time and again, to reach a duck, and repeat the process to bring the duck back to shore. That takes courage, super-dog strength, and a love of the retrieving game. These reports may be authentic, or they may be exaggerated a bit to add color. In any case, the dog has guts, style, and endurance.

It is unlikely that any retriever will ever match the swimming ability of a healthy, well-conditioned Chessie. There are dozens of reports of this dog swimming a mile to retrieve a single duck. Commercial waterfowlers would routinely send a Chesapeake to retrieve two hundred ducks in one night of good shooting. When one considers that these feats were carried out in the rough waters of Chesapeake Bay, it is no wonder that the breed is renowned for its swimming ability and stamina.

Coat

An outer coat that is harsh and oily aids the Chessie's swimming ability. Its undercoat is quite thick, fine, wooly, and oily as well. Petting a Chessie will result in a waxy deposit on your fingers. It is this oil that retains the dog's body heat, resists water, and prevents the Chesapeake from getting wet to the skin. The coat of a Chesapeake is unique. If it looks like that of any other breed, it isn't a good Chesapeake coat. It should be springy over the entire body due to the soft wooly undercoat. The outer coat has a wavy or crinkled appearance, but it should never be curly.

This unique coat is not composed of two sets of hairs, but results from the differences in texture and the deposition of pigment along the hair. The section of hair that is close to the skin has a relatively small amount of pigment, which is distributed evenly along the shaft. The section of hair that is closest to the tip contains clumps of pigment that gives the hair a harsh, water-resistant quality and the "dead-grass" color that is also unique to this breed. The coat color is said to be "self-colored," which means that a single pigment is involved, but it may vary in concentration.

Memory and Reasoning Power

Most dogs are known to possess cognitive thought processes by which they solve problems. They are capable of drawing conclusions based on their judgment. One typical Chesapeake characteristic is an outstanding memory. Once having learned what you want, the Chessie isn't likely to ever forget. Double and triple retrieves are no problem for this dog. The command "*Mark*" is given to a retriever to call her attention to the bird that the hunter hopes to shoot. The dog must then mentally mark the spot where the bird falls. Some exceptional Chessies can mark as many as five or six downed birds and retrieve them, without forgetting one.

Jump shooting is a sport that requires both a good marksman and an alert dog. It is quite different from blind shooting or upland hunting with a

Ethel raced the duck downstream until she was ahead of it, then hit the water to make the retrieve.

pointer or setter. The hunter walks along a river or field with the retriever following a step behind. When a bird breaks cover or leaves the water, the hunter quickly tells the dog to *mark* and instantly aims and shoots. This is a sport that is difficult to match when you own a Chessie. It is awesome to watch this dog outsmart the rapids by running down the bank, then charging the water, leaping far out into the rushing current, plummeting through the ice, and picking the fowl from the water as you might pluck a rubber duck from your bathtub.

Sometimes an incident occurs to illustrate how intelligent this dog is and how it is always thinking. It is a tribute to fine training to be sure, but is also an indication of the dog's reasoning and memory.

My two sons and I were jump shooting ducks on the Roaring Fork River. Champion Snocre's Excess Baggage, a big, beautiful Chessie that we called Ethel, was retrieving for us on this cold, snowy Colorado morning. Shortly after daylight, she swam the

Chessies are very accomplished swimmers.

ten feet of shallow water to a small ice-fringed and snow-covered island, accompanying her handler Tim, who wore hip waders. Tapering ice extended sharply about four feet into the swift current on the far side of the island. As Tim and Ethel stepped around the little hill on the island, three gigantic mallard drakes suddenly rose into the frigid morning. They flew vertically into the air from a point about twenty yards in front of Tim and Ethel. Purely by chance, Tim's first shot caught two of the ducks in alignment and downed both of them, but one was obviously only winged. His second shot sent the third greenhead into the water further downstream.

Tim was taken by surprise by the ducks' rapid ascent from the island and didn't have time to tell Ethel to *mark* before he shouldered his 12-gauge and pulled the trigger, but that was usually an irrelevant command to the dog anyway. Without being told to fetch, Ethel hit full stride immediately after the two shots and plunged off the snowy bank, crashing through two or three inches of ice. She swam into the current, disappeared beneath the water a couple of times, and brought up the wounded bird. She struggled to find footing on the thin ice as she returned the wounded drake to Tim, where she hurriedly dropped it at his feet. She didn't break stride as she made a long dash down the island, the powdery snow flying above her head. She sped downstream, well ahead of the second bird that bobbed swiftly along in the fast water. Ethel dove into the icy river again, picked up the duck, swam to the frozen ring around the island, fought her way through the ice, and unceremoniously dumped the bird at Tim's feet.

Her momentum was hardly interrupted as she again pivoted and ran full tilt through the fresh snow until she came to the end of the little island. Without hesitation, she leaped into the water, swam to the riverbank, and ran sixty or more yards down the bank through foot-deep snow. She broke through the ice once more as she hit the river at full speed, swimming crosscurrent to intercept the remaining duck.

She took her time trotting to Tim, who had left the island to join us. We stood in openmouthed astonishment at this dog's intelligence, talent, persistence, and stamina. She then performed according to her training. She approached Tim slowly and, when directly in front of him, she sat and looked up at him with the duck in her mouth, as if to say "It's all in a day's work."

It has been said that the Chesapeake Bay Retriever is superior to any breed on earth in its ability to stand climatic punishment in heavy seas and zero degree weather. That claim was made over a century and a half ago, but it is still true today when hunting conditions demand superior courage, intelligence, and stamina. The venerable Chesapeake is tough to the bone, with sufficient endurance to withstand the most severe hunting conditions and the roughest water.

Popularity As a Competition Dog

The Chesapeake is a show dog, but not usually at the expense of its working ability. The breed was developed as a hardy, cold-proof water retriever with an excellent nose, without regard for its status in a show ring. The hunters of the early days weren't interested in dog shows; to breed dogs for bench shows seemed to be a waste of good hunting stock.

The first American Chesapeake Club (ACC) retriever trial was held in 1932. In those days, actual hunting was part of a field trial but the trial soon became a game unto itself and professional handler-trainers took the place of hunters and retriever owners.

Year by year, this breed has become more popular in obedience work and tracking trial competitions. Agility trials are another type of competition that have recently attracted the fun-loving Chessie as well.

The Chessie remains the ultimate water retriever, and the ACC awards Working Dog (WD) and Working Dog Excellent (WDX) titles to dogs that have passed retrieving tests on land and in water.

Dual-Purpose Dog?

The Chesapeake is a sporting dog that is not generally considered a dual-purpose breed in the same sense that the German Shorthaired Pointer or Brittany is. Those breeds are basically land retrievers that exhibit well in field trials and conformation shows, and many hold the coveted title of dual champion. There are some dual champions in the Chesapeake ranks, and this dog continues to excel as a

Coats are self-colored in various shades of "dead grass."

show dog while retaining its superb hunter status in the field. In 1996, the American Kennel Club (AKC) awarded 104 Junior Hunter, 22 Senior Hunter, and 11 Master Hunter titles to representatives of the Chesapeake breed.

Show History

The Chessie isn't considered by many to be a gorgeous dog. It lacks the flowing grace of the setters and its coat is less luxurious than that of some of the spaniels.

Chessies were awarded 106 Champion of Record titles by the AKC in 1996. In 1995, 125 were awarded, and 121 in 1994. Their Sporting Group and Best of Show wins are far less regular.

The breed is judged against its own standard, and there is a great effort to preserve the "duck dog" image of the Chessie. In the conformation standard, more emphasis is given to coat quality than to any feathering or flourishes. The dog's strength, balance, soundness, and disposition are more important than esoteric factors. Its intelligence, love

Chessies prefer hunting and swimming but they also make excellent family dogs.

of water, and willingness to work are stressed in the breed standard.

In 1989, about a century after the breed's first appearance in the AKC registry, there were 4,427 purebred Chesapeakes registered, making them forty-second in popularity among the 130 breeds then registered by the AKC. By 1996, the number of Chessies registered had risen to 5,540, with their popularity remaining forty-second out of a total of 143 breeds registered by the AKC. Chesapeakes are the eighth most popular sporting dog in the United States in a field of 24 breeds.

Extraordinary Hunters

Some other sporting breeds excel in field trials and dog shows, but have forgotten their heritage that was founded on the lakes and waterways of our nation. Not so the Chesapeake. As a gundog, the Chessie is usually soft-mouthed and easily trained, although in the past some were said to be both stubborn and hard-mouthed. These inexcusable traits are not typical of today's Chessie.

Rarely are two dogs needed for a party of hunters; the Chesapeake will easily retrieve for three shooters in a blind or walking. This tireless retriever can also be used on upland birds with fairly uniform results. It typically doesn't point or set land birds, but its ability to locate them in heavy cover is remarkable. It will not take a backseat to any dog when retrieving a downed bird, whether on land or in water.

Family Dog

Although it is true that the Chessie would rather be hunting or swimming, it is a loyal and faithful family dog, regardless of how it is otherwise used.

Because the Chessie is so tough and hardy, it is sometimes described as a thickheaded dog. Nonsense. This dog is sensitive, clever, quite intelligent, gentle, happy, and fun loving, but the Chessie must understand what is expected of it. The Chesapeake is a bright, resourceful dog that is anxious to please its family. These dogs love life and people; they will do anything to please their owners.

In spite of stories to the contrary, the friendly Chessie doesn't respond well to rough treatment. This breed is not easy to force. It will usually accept correction from its trainer, unless the trainer crosses the fine line between correction and abuse. Like other dogs, the Chessie can be led or driven, and it is the general opinion that the dog will respond better to leading.

The average Chessie tends to be a one-man dog in the field, but at home it may pay more attention to the children of the family. The Chessie will usually favor those individuals who spend the most time training and disciplining it. Consistency, guidance, and training are very important to this dog. The Chesapeake is a strong, tough dog with a gentle disposition and a gigantic heart, and it is best suited to a home with active, mild-tempered, patient owners.

Although there are exceptions to the rule, most breeders agree that the Chessie is not typically aggressive. A Chessie will usually pay more attention to its handler in the field than to other dogs in the area. Males and females alike are tolerant, if not friendly, with other dogs. A Chesapeake is dominant, rather than aggressive. It will rarely start a fight, but can unquestionably take care of itself if challenged by another dog. The Chessie doesn't seem to have a killer instinct, but usually fights by running into its opponent, driving a massive shoulder into the quarrelsome dog to send it rolling. Then the powerful Chessie will stand over the other dog growling its message until its ultimatum has been accepted.

This breed is not for everyone. Chessies are not cookie-cutter dogs; there are no two exactly alike and each has a singular personality. Their tolerance for pain is quite high, which allows some trainers to take advantage of them. When their confidence is gained with love, patience, and kindness, their loyalty will be your reward.

Chessie breeders describe their dogs as easy as most other breeds to housebreak. They make great pets for kids, and love to tag about with them every day. They are at their very best when they are a member of the family and are included in family activities. They are wonderful, natural watchdogs and are very protective of their family and possessions. According to most breeders, a Chessie will excel in showing, fieldwork, hunting, or obedience, depending on the owner's skill and interest in training. The general feeling is that if Chessies are bred to meet the standard, they will do well in any endeavor they are set to.

Unless we take responsibility for stewardship of our dogs, they will find their way into shelters.

More than one owner takes the Chessie from field competition on one day, brushes the dog out, and enters it in a conformation show the next day. At night, the same dog may be found sleeping at the foot of some little boy's bed.

Human Stewardship

Dog management is a great responsibility, one that is often neglected. People see a strong, well-trained dog and admire its beautiful coat, quiet personality, and superb intelligence. They assume that all dogs of that breed somehow grow up to be quiet and wonderfully obedient. They fail to realize that to produce this admired dog, untold hours were invested in its care and hundreds of dollars were spent for specialized education and training. These naïve observers rush out and buy a puppy of the same breed and a year later the dog has become a nuisance or a liability, through no fault of its own. This lack of planning has led to the destruction of millions of beautiful canine pets that were thoughtlessly obtained by well-meaning families.

Unfortunately, every breed is occasionally caught up in this unfortunate scenario. Too often, good intentions, the reputation of the breed, or the

Substituting quail for ducks is OK for an old Ethel.

of managers when we obtain a dog. That is critically important, whether shopping for a purebred Chessie or a mixed-breed pup for a child's pet.

A neutering policy should be employed for all pets that breeders sell, with sales contracts to enforce the policy. Prospective breeders must be made aware that only proven dogs should be used in a breeding program. Careless owners and breeders who assume that all registered dogs are breeding quality exacerbate the dog overpopulation problem.

If you find yourself with a Chessie that you can't keep, contact the Chesapeake club in your area or the American Chesapeake Club. (See Useful Addresses and Literature, page 99.)

Think Before You Buy

Before embarking on your Chesapeake shopping trip, remember that this breed isn't the ideal dog for every family, regardless of its exceptional qualities. You should never purchase any dog, least of all a Chessie, on a whim. The Chesapeake's heritage is that of a hunting dog and can't be compared to small house pets that require minimal exercise or attention. Generalizations have been made about the Chesapeake breed but you must realize that every Chessie doesn't fit these descriptions. They aren't cloned to have identical personalities and aptitudes. They have individual characteristics that can be molded to some extent, but they are strong-willed dogs that possess separate, distinctive attitudes. Because your Chesapeake is an active dog, time and space must be provided for it to expend that energy. Unless you lead an active, outdoor life and plan to spend a great deal of time with your new Chessie, maybe you should rethink your selection.

adorable face of a Chessie puppy leads a family to purchase a pup. The tragic end to this story is that a year later the energetic but bored dog winds up in the dog warden's truck or in a kennel operated by a rescue organization.

Unclaimed or unwanted American pets now number in the hundreds of thousands. Rejected dogs fill the pounds, breed rescue service kennels, and animal shelters across the country. When those facilities can no longer house them, they are euthanatized (put to sleep) in enormous numbers.

Stewardship, "the careful and responsible management of something that is entrusted to one's care," is the answer to this problem. All of us who obtain dogs and do not have them sexually neutered before they reach reproductive age are poor stewards. Nearly as negligent are those of us who adopt a dog and fail to train it, teach it manners, and give it something to do. We must accept the role

Selecting Your Chessie

Are You Ready for a Dog?

Before deciding on a Chesapeake, there are a few questions you should ask yourself regarding a new dog in the family. Buying a pet on impulse usually leads to disappointment that can be disastrous. Owning a dog for any reason requires a long-term commitment that deserves careful thought by its owners. This puppy will share your home and heart for many years and the decision to obtain it should be discussed with, and clearly understood by, all household members. A simplified checklist follows with many items to consider before purchasing a new dog.

• Do you have time to spend with a new pet? Unfortunately, this item is frequently overlooked, especially if there are young children in the family. Grown-ups often make the mistake of delegating a puppy's care to a four- or five-year-old child. That is unfair to both the child and the puppy. If you are to be happy with your dog, you must be ready to give the dog many hours of your attention.

• Do you have physical space for a dog? In most cases, that means at least a fenced yard and a warm, dry doghouse. If the Chessie pup is going to share your home, do you have an area to dedicate to its use during the period of housebreaking?

• Can you afford a dog? The purchase price is only the beginning of dog ownership. There are annual vaccinations to pay for and neutering or spaying fees to consider. Every dog, even under the best circumstances, will occasionally require veterinary assistance. Call a veterinarian and get an average per year cost for medical maintenance for the dog. Your Chessie will deserve the best food. Tick, flea, and heartworm control must also be provided. Finally, consider the cost of dishes, beds, collars, and leashes.

• Can you afford specialized training? If you plan to enter your Chessie in retriever trials, have you calculated the cost of a professional handler? Maintaining a competitive field trial dog is a major project with a major cost.

• Are you frequently away from home? Have you investigated boarding kennels or do you have reliable friends who will care for your Chesapeake when you are away?

Timing

Failing to plan often has the same results as planning to fail. In order to get a pup started correctly, everyone in the family must be ready for it. Don't buy your puppy immediately before the holidays. Confusion reigns in most households around Christmas time and the pup may be neglected in the rush. A preferred plan is to purchase dog equipment and a picture of the pup to place under the Christmas tree. Bring the puppy home later, after the holiday is past, the guests are gone, and the family has settled into its normal routine.

Do you usually take a vacation in the summer? If you plan to be gone the first few weeks of July, don't select your new pup in May or June. You must be at home to properly train a puppy and you can't delegate this

Puppies shouldn't be given as Christmas surprises.

responsibility to a friend or boarding kennel. Consistency is the key to housebreaking and leash training, and it is better not to interrupt it for weeks at a time.

School children usually change their routine during spring break and sometimes guests and parties throw the household into confusion. Don't bring a new puppy into that atmosphere. Extra people to play with the pup might seem like a good idea, but they might inadvertently introduce undesirable habits to your puppy.

Is a Chessie the Right Dog?

A Non-Slip Retriever

There are basically three types of retrievers. The first is a pointer or setter, which retrieves after locating and pointing a bird for the handler to shoot. The second type is a "nose hunter," or one that is taken to the field to find the scent of game that has been wounded and can't be located. This exercise is often referred to as a "dead hunt." The third is a non-slip retriever. This term is usually used to describe a duck dog that works at the handler's heel or slightly behind the handler, and retrieves the game when it is shot. It doesn't typically point or flush live birds, but is primarily one that retrieves game after it as been shot. This type includes the Chesapeake.

Whether you are a sportsman or a conservationist, guns and the use of guns to provide game meat for our tables is a part of our national heritage, an integral part of the American culture. Retrievers of all three types were originally bred to augment the efforts of commercial hunters and sportsmen. Retrievers continue to contribute to the conservation of our natural game resources. Without trained retrievers, many thousands of game birds would be lost. That is sufficient reason for the existence of retrievers.

A well-trained Chesapeake will carry a raw egg in its mouth and place it in your hand without cracking it. The birds it retrieves don't suffer from being handled by its soft mouth. A Chesapeake's activities as a member of a hunting team assures that all birds are quickly delivered to the handler. The value of a good nose can't be appreciated until your Chessie has successfully scented out and retrieved a few birds from dense cover or has picked them from fast-moving water—birds that would be wasted without the help of a retriever. The retriever is a specialist, a game conservationist of the finest variety.

Popularity

There were 1,319 Chesapeake litters registered by the AKC in 1996, and that number has been relatively constant for the past several years. Compare that figure to the Golden Retriever with 18,566 litters registered or the Labrador Retriever registration of nearly 39,000 litters. This modest but constant number of Chesapeake litters indicates a continued interest in the breed in the United States, but not an oversupply of puppies. When breeds become number one in popularity, they often attract too much attention and are overbred. The Chessie hasn't risen to those popularity heights yet; hopefully it never will. For the most part, responsible breeders still maintain good control over this breed, but remember, buying a good dog requires a fair amount of knowledge and research. There are unscrupulous breeders who produce Chessies with terrible temperaments, bad conformation, and with virtually no hunting skills. All Chessies, unfortunately, are not the same; some fall far short of the ideal dog described here.

Health and Life Expectancy

Chessies, being among the larger and heavier hunting breeds, are usually destined to live shorter lives than the small terriers and lapdogs. It isn't uncommon, however, to have your Chesapeake for 10 to 13 years; a few live even longer. The key to good health and longevity for a dog isn't much different from our own. A preventive medicine program that is followed throughout life is of utmost importance.

Proper nutrition is critically important to your pet's longevity, as is the protection afforded by a kennel or yard confinement. Grooming and coat care is fundamental to a dog's general health.

Chessies are active, intelligent pets and special attention should be given to keeping them as busy as possible. If you hunt, exercise may not be a problem, but if your hunting is only done for a few hours on an occasional weekend, that may not supply enough exercise for a Chessie. In the cases of companions and conformation show dogs, you must arrange regular playtimes or your Chessie will become bored and develop nuisance habits such as chewing, digging, or barking.

Walks with the dog and regular playtimes can't be overdone.

Veterinary Opinion

In order to choose the right dog for your family, consult with knowledgeable people. Talk with a veterinarian about your choice of breed. In all probability, the veterinarian has had experience with Chessies and will be able to provide insights on your selection. Veterinarians' opinions are invaluable; they handle dogs by the dozens every day, and have firsthand experience with the idiosyncrasies of many breeds.

A pre-purchase discussion with your veterinarian serves many purposes. You can gain a general idea of the expense involved in routine dog care. Boarding kennels that are available in the area can be discussed. Risks of certain diseases that are indigenous to your region of the country may be brought to your attention. Hereditary conditions that are prevalent in Chesapeake Bay Retrievers can be outlined and you may receive advice on how to detect commonly recognized problems. A veterinarian may even be able to recommend Chessie breeders, owners, and trainers in your locality.

Choosing the Right Chessie

Male or Female?

Both male and female Chessies are strong, loyal, trainable, affectionate, and playful. There is very little difference in the sexes when looking for a pet or hunter that is to be neutered at or before adulthood. If a female is chosen, the cost of spaying might be a bit more than the cost of castration of a male, but when prorated over the life of the dog, that is a minor consideration. Both sexes may be trained with the same degree of success. Chesapeakes, whether male or female, are quick to learn, eager to please, and require minimum correction.

Who could resist this Chessie pup?

If you plan to show or enter your Chessie in retriever trials and hunting tests, do you also plan to raise puppies? If so, a show-quality female is your obvious choice. Few males are good enough to be considered stud dogs, and even if you have a male that wins his share of ribbons, he isn't likely to be in great demand for breeding.

Appropriate Age to Acquire a Puppy

Canine mothers often stop feeding their brood by six weeks of age. Prior to that time, and for a couple of weeks after weaning, the pups learn to socialize with their dam and siblings. It is a serious mistake to remove them from this environment before that time. From birth to eight weeks, while associating with their littermates, they learn valuable lessons about getting along with other dogs.

Most breeders will keep puppies until they are at least seven weeks old, and you should try to bring the pup into your home as soon as possible after that age. The socialization period of puppies and humans extends from shortly after birth to three months of age. It is during this important bonding time that the pup should be introduced to humans. That is the period when they will best learn vital lessons that stay with them the rest of their lives. Puppies often learn leash manners at six to eight weeks. The time before 12 weeks is also when bad habits may be learned and those, too, are deeply imprinted in puppy minds.

If for some reason you aren't able to bring your Chessie home before it is three months old, choose a puppy that has been handled as much as possible by the breeder's family. Pups that mature without human companionship and are kept exclusively with other dogs during their early life may not bond to their owners readily and may prove to be poor companions. Chessies are, however, very human-

There is no appreciable difference in the health care costs, provided that your pup is to be spayed or castrated. If you are considering showing your Chessie in conformation or field trials, it can't be neutered, and you must remember that females come in heat twice a year. You can enjoy recreational hunting, obedience, agility, tracking, and 4-H competition with a neutered Chesapeake.

Some of us appreciate the temperament of females; others prefer masculine characteristics. Male dogs in general tend to be more aggressive than females, and this deserves consideration. Do you have other male dogs in the household? If so, that could present a problem unless the males are raised together or neutered, and even neutering won't necessarily stop male aggression. Females are usually more gentle than males, but this too is relative. Hunting and swimming is the Chesapeake's life; eagerness to work and play will dominate both sexes.

oriented dogs; with love and attention, they will usually bond with an attentive and caring family.

Temperament

It's often difficult to identify personality differences among puppies in a litter of playful, frisky youngsters, but don't overlook temperament when choosing a pup. The dam and sire will often give you a general idea of what their offsprings' attitude will be like when they grow up. Shy dogs don't usually make good hunters or companions, or at best they are more difficult to train and handle. Viciousness isn't a typical trait of Chesapeake Bay Retrievers, but stay away from puppies whose sire or dam is quarrelsome, belligerent, and difficult to handle. The Chessie has the distinction of being labeled as the surliest sporting dog breed. This is a reputation that is being slowly changed by intelligent breeding, showing, and recognition in obedience and agility work. There is no excuse for buying a dog from parents that display a bad attitude.

Type of Chessie

Gundogs

When choosing a gundog, similar guidelines should be employed as when choosing a companion or show dog, but with a few added requirements. Working Dog Certificates that have been awarded to the sire and dam are a reliable indication that the puppy is from gundog lines. Usually these puppies will be exposed to guns and gunfire at a fairly early age, and certainly before they are sold as hunting prospects. They should have a keen interest in retrieving. At 6 to 12 weeks of age, they should pick up and carry a ball, dummy, sock, or bird wing. Many retrievers are started on live, netted birds before they are weaned, but a potential gundog can't be critically eval-

Selection should be a careful process.

uated by his retrieving interest or ability as a pup. Most Chessies will retrieve anything they can pick up whether or not they are the progeny of proven gundogs. Probably the most reliable measure of a gundog at the age of seven weeks is the performance of its parents and grandparents.

Field Trial Dogs

If you wish to purchase a Chessie to compete in formal retriever trials and hunting tests, the best advice is to seek better advice than you can find in any book. Talk to individuals who are involved with retriever trials. Take their advice regarding kennels that participate in trials and run winning dogs. Seek out the advice of a professional trainer. Contact one of the retriever clubs (see Useful Addresses and Literature, page 99). Attend retriever trials and meet the people who participate. Watch the field Chessies perform and talk to their owners. The AKC or ACC can refer you to competition retriever trials in your region.

HOW-TO:
Perform an On-the-Spot Health Inspection

It's difficult to be objective when the entire litter is friendly and happy.

Even a novice can inspect a pup and make a rough evaluation of its health, personality, and conformation to the Chesapeake standard. You should do so before choosing a pet to share your life for the next dozen years.

Remember that it is impossible to pick a good pup from a poor litter. If you see an assortment of skinny, runny-eyed, lethargic, coughing puppies, don't even pick one up. Don't make the mistake of taking a sick pup home with the guarantee that it will get better in a day or two. Don't buy a puppy that is receiving medication. Wait until a veterinarian has pronounced the pup healthy. Everyone is entitled to begin his or her relationship with a healthy dog—don't settle for less!

Look at the puppies' surroundings. If there are dirty food dishes lying about, overturned water bowls, and other signs of poor sanitation, beware! If confined to a yard, look for old feces scattered about or uneaten food that attracts flies.

Your pup is a reflection of its parents. If only the dam is present, ask to see a picture of the sire, and if possible, pictures of his other progeny. Don't rule a litter out because of the dam's physical condition. A good dam may look a bit run-down after weaning a litter of fat little Chessie pups. She may have a sagging stomach, be thinner than normal, and have a poor coat when you see her. However, she should be clean, active, friendly, and inquisitive. Look at her puppies from previous litters if any are available.

The personality of the dam and sire is a vital part of puppy selection. If the adults are shy, timid, or reluctant to be handled, their puppies will probably have similar attitudes. If they are quarrelsome or belligerent, better look somewhere else for your Chessie.

When looking at pups that are about eight to ten weeks old, you will make a more intelligent choice if you follow these guidelines.
• Stand back and observe the litter from a few yards away. See if there are puppies that are reluctant to be picked up or petted. Make mental note of those that aren't joining in the tumbling and play. Perhaps one or two will run to hide behind their dam or nesting box. Those pups are often insecure and are probably too young to leave their dam and siblings. Visit the litter more than once if the pups seem timid; a few days at this age make a big difference.
• Choose a puppy that is inquisitive and affectionate, but one that isn't aggressively attacking its siblings. Try to concentrate on pups that are anxious to meet you rather than hanging back. A certain amount of fear is normal when a stranger approaches a puppy, but don't

The parents of a pup are one indication of how the puppy will develop and what its personality will be.

choose a pup that is overtly shy.
• After you have narrowed the selection process to one pup, squat or sit on the floor and carefully pick Rowdy up. It is important to make yourself as small as possible when you first approach him. Lying down on the floor or lawn (if practical) is an excellent posture to take. Don't grab a puppy as it runs by, and don't corner it somewhere. If the breeder's family has handled the pups, Rowdy will catch you; you won't have to chase him.

Reject a pup that immediately takes a defensive stance when you reach for it. If it snaps, screams, or otherwise seems frightened, it is probably not the pup for you.

Take Rowdy into another room or away from the rest of the litter; sit on the floor and watch his attitude when you set him beside you. If one end is still wagging and the other is licking your face, you are nearing a good selection.
• Cradle him in your arms in an upside-down position and scratch his tummy and chin. He should allow that with little objection and without squirming to right himself.
• After you have made friendly overtures to Rowdy for a few minutes while sitting on the floor, stand him upright on your lap. Open his mouth and check his bite. The upper incisor teeth should overlap and touch the lower front teeth. Any amount of gap between the upper and lower teeth (overshot or undershot) is a serious fault in Chesapeake Bay Retrievers and should affect your choice, especially if you are looking for a dog to show or breed. A slight

Holding the puppy in your arms indicates his willingness to be handled.

bite fault should not be a consideration if the puppy is purchased as a pet or gundog that will be neutered. He can still be entered in several competitions; his deformity won't interfere with eating, and it rarely causes any health problems.
• With Rowdy standing or sitting, feel his abdomen for evidence of an umbilical hernia. A hernia may be identified as a protrusion of tissue, about the size of a marble, at the site of his navel. When the puppy is seven or eight weeks old, hernias are soft and when pressed, they may disappear into the abdomen. Hernias are easily

Check the puppy's eyes for mattering.

repaired, but they represent an additional expense to you.
• If selecting a male, check for the presence of testicles. They should be descended into his scrotum by eight or ten weeks of age, and if not, they might never descend. That doesn't present a serious problem in a companion animal or a gundog, but if you are considering entering your Chessie in competition, either leave the pup in the kennel until the testicles drop into place, or pick another pup. (See Cryptorchidism, page 85, in the health care chapter.)
• Look at the puppy's eyes; they should be set wide apart and should be clear, not mattering or squinting. The puppy may be six to eight months old before the amber eye color is seen. The color of the eyes isn't terribly important in pets, but for show purposes, a yellowish or dark amber color is preferred. The best indications of adult eye color are the parents.
• The Chesapeake coat color is very important. Dead grass is the term that describes a good Chessie's color. It may vary from tan to dark brown, and it is permissible to have small white spots on its chest, belly, or toes, but the less white that is seen the better.
• The nose rubber should be moist. Dry nostrils with matter caked in the corners are sure signs of health problems.
• The dewclaws should have been removed at about three days of age. If they are still present on either hind legs or forelegs, it isn't a serious problem, because they can be surgically removed at any time. This can mean an expense for you.

Show Dogs

Conformation show dogs will probably be available from the same kennels that produce retriever trial dogs. If a breeding kennel displays on its walls ribbons and rosettes from AKC shows, and the dogs that won those awards are living in their kennels, you have a better than average chance of acquiring a show dog.

Out of every litter of eight Chesapeake puppies from "show" parents, perhaps only one or two puppies are destined to have any career on the show circuit. The breeder often keeps those puppies until they are three or four months of age to watch their development. Remember, there really shouldn't be any notable difference between show-quality puppies and those that are destined to hunt. Kennels that raise field dogs should be able to supply your need for a show dog and vice versa.

Companion Dogs

Today, 30 to 60 percent of the Chessie pups that are whelped are sold as pets and companions. Although at first glance it seems a shame to consign a wonderful duck dog to a backyard where it never has the opportunity to retrieve game, the Chesapeake doesn't seem to mind. This dog has been bred for generations to hunt, but like most other hunting breeds, its personality is malleable and it will adapt to the lifestyle of a family pet quite well.

Any Chessie breeder may supply pets. Every litter includes some pups that don't quite measure up to the requirements of competition, conformation show, or hunting dogs. Rowdy's pedigree may be stippled with Champions that indicate careful breeding, but perhaps he has some color or conformational fault that isn't conducive to a performance career. Such a pup may be sold for less than the choice puppies, but he will have all of the fundamental characteristics of those pups and should be a wonderful companion.

Finding the Right Breeder

Breeders may be located in a number of ways. The American Chesapeake Club (ACC) is a fine place to start. Write to the club secretary, or contact the AKC for the name of the current national or regional club secretary (see Useful Addresses and Literature, page 99). Ask for a list of ACC members in your locality. The AKC has a Web page that may be accessed to find breed club secretaries and other information. The E-mail address is http://AKC.org.

To meet Chesapeake fanciers, go to a dog show in your region. Attend retriever trials, hunting tests, and agility and obedience trials where you can make contacts that are invaluable if you are looking for a performance dog. Various dog magazines usually carry advertisements for Chessies. Information about shows and trials may be obtained from the *American Kennel Club Gazette*, a monthly publication of the AKC. (See Useful Addresses and Literature, page 100.)

Find a good breeder and you will probably find a good puppy.

It also contains a breed listing with many kennel advertisements.

Remember that if you look for Chessie ads in your local newspaper, you might be looking for trouble! Legitimate breeders occasionally advertise in newspapers, but a back-yard breeder who isn't interested in the betterment of the breed will often place a newspaper ad. These ads also may promote puppies that originate in puppy mills.

Puppy mills are establishments that own bitches of various breeds, and produce hundreds of pups a year. They are notorious for producing poor-quality pups with questionable health and parentage. It is easy to spot a puppy factory. When you arrive, a litter may be presented without the dam. If you ask to see her, an excuse is usually made, or if you see her, she may be in pitiful condition. If you gain entrance to the kennel, you will usually see various breeds, crowded and dirty conditions, very little provision for exercise, and thin, overworked dams. Pups from these puppy mills should be avoided at all costs.

Pet stores may be a viable option for you, but they usually don't have the dam or sire of a pup, and rarely can you see the puppy's siblings. However, many pet stores now maintain pedigrees and complete records of the puppies' origin and you are often able to learn the name of the kennel that raised the pup and satisfy your requirements.

Neighborhood litters offer a source of companion dogs that is questionable at best. Before you buy a back-yard breeder's Chessie, be sure to examine the AKC registration and pedigree of the dam and sire. If the puppies aren't registered, or if their parents are less than two years old, beware! More is said about the importance of certification of normal hips in

These two Silvercreek Chessies have brightened the day for this nursing home resident.

the section on hereditary conditions (see Canine Hip Dysplasia, page 86). Backyard-bred puppies are often less expensive than kennel-raised dogs, and may prove to be fine pets, but it is unlikely that you will receive guarantees of any kind.

Parents are a good indication of what the pup will look like.

Health Records

You have found the perfect puppy. Rowdy is a bundle of energy and he appears hale and healthy. What else do you need? There are a number of documents that should accompany your new Chessie. Among them are records of when and by whom the pup was vaccinated, the product used, and when another vaccination is due.

The date a worm check was done and the results of the fecal exam should be included, together with the date of treatment for the parasites if the fecal exam was positive. The health papers should specify what product was administered and the dose that was given.

The records should include the dates of health examinations, and the name and address of the veterinarian who performed the examinations. If the pup was seen for an illness, that should be specified, as well as the name and dosage of medication used.

If heartworm, tick, or flea preventive medication has been started, the dates and the product used should be noted.

The pup's diet should be recorded, including the quantity, brand name, and frequency of feeding.

Breeders should have this information readily available, and usually more; be sure you receive it in writing. Continued preventive health care depends on complete health records.

AKC Papers

If the pup's parents are registered with the AKC, you should receive the puppy litter registration at the time you take Rowdy home. If you are buying a pet-quality pup, the breeder may choose to withhold the registration papers until proof of neutering the puppy is furnished. The registration may likewise be retained until the final payment is received if you have contracted to pay for the pup in installments.

If AKC registration is not available from the breeder, you are in a buyer-beware situation. The AKC is not a regulatory agency. It can't get your money back, and you might need to resort to small claims court to obtain satisfaction. If you decide to buy the pup anyway, be sure to get a bill of sale from the breeder. This bill of sale should include the name and AKC registration numbers of the sire and dam, the dates of breeding, the date of whelping, and the names and phone numbers of the owners of both sire and dam.

A pedigree is a record of several generations of the puppy's ancestors. It has no particular value in pet-quality pups, but is very significant if you have purchased a competition dog or if you intend to breed it. A pedigree is no better than its source, and one is available from the AKC for a fee if you are able to furnish the registration number.

If either you or the seller have negotiated any special considerations that apply to the purchase, put those terms in writing. If you agree to spay or castrate the pup by a certain age, write it down. If the breeder guarantees the puppy to be in good health, get that in writing, together with the duration of the guarantee. Most breeders will replace a pup if it has a disease or deformity that is discovered by your veterinarian. Be sure that the terms of the guarantee clearly specify whether it assures you of your money back, or a replacement pup.

Taking Your Chesapeake Puppy Home

First Days in Your Home

The first days of dog ownership are stressful for both the pet and owner. Depending on her age, Rosie must be fed several meals per day at regular intervals. If she is kept in the house, she must be taken outside for eliminations. You must make allowances for Rosie's exercise needs by including walks and playtimes in your daily plans. There are physical and emotional demands on your lives that were not previously present.

Diet

Change initiates stresses, even if they aren't readily perceived. When Rosie arrives in your home, minimize those stresses by following the previously established feeding program. If you wish to change her diet to a better quality food, wait a week. After a week or two in your home, you can make those changes slowly by mixing the new product with the previous food in gradually increasing amounts. Maintenance dietary recommendations are found in Feeding Your Chesapeake, beginning on page 50.

Bonding and Socialization

Human bonding and family adjustment occur rapidly in a young Chessie puppy. During the first weeks, Rosie will form lifelong relationships with her human companions. She will accept correction quickly and easily; the lessons taught will be promptly imprinted on her personality. This is the prime time to establish your love and devotion to your new pet, and Rosie will reciprocate. She will bond quickly to the person(s) who train, play with, and discipline her. As she becomes familiar with the household routine, Rosie will quickly recognize the restrictions placed upon her.

Chessie puppies are amazingly tolerant of children, and when tormented by a toddler, Rosie will probably move away. Young people should always be supervised and instructed to handle the pup gently; rough play shouldn't be

Be sure that the kennel and run are of adequate size for an adult Chessie.

Well-mannered dogs are no accident.

tion during that developmental period is essential. Raising a Chessie puppy isn't a spectator sport. Rosie will learn the rules of the household only if you interact with her daily. At the same time, you will learn about Rosie's character—her likes, dislikes, and the things that satisfy her the most. You can use this knowledge to great advantage when her training is begun.

Necessary Quarters

Rosie is probably destined to be a family pet, and will spend a good deal of time inside your house. Perhaps you already have a fenced yard and expect her to have the run of the yard and sleep in your home at night. Those accommodations are fine, providing you have taken a few preliminary precautions to protect both your puppy and your property.

Kennel and Run

If your yard fence is only 3 or 4 feet (1–1.2 m) tall, an outdoor kennel is essential. Locate Rosie's kennel in an area that slopes gently downward from front to back. A few inches or even a foot of slope makes for good drainage away from the front of the run, where she will spend most of her time. That is particularly important if your home is in a rainy environment. A 6-foot (2-m) chain-link fence will serve your needs well. If possible, place it in the shade of trees and make the run as large as possible. Most kennel runs are not adequate to provide ample exercise space for an athletic Chessie, and should be used only as a place to safely house Rosie when you are away. The run should be large enough to allow the dog to move about freely, and it should be located where shade from the sun is always available.

An elevated wooden platform, large enough to allow an adult Chesapeake to stretch out, should be built under and in front of the doghouse. The platform

tolerated. Within a few weeks, Rosie will be anxious to please. She will learn to recognize her toys and to anticipate the ball games and hide-and-seek exercises. Worn-out socks with a knot tied in them are excellent chew toys for a young Chessie. When Rosie begins to mouth your hands, legs, or furniture, substitute a knotted sock and praise her as she carries it about.

For the first few months, puppies require a great deal of personal attention and time commitment. At seven, eight, or nine weeks of age, they are typical lovable, mischievous puppies. They play, chew, run, and romp with children or adults, and grow like weeds. They metamorphose from little balls of puppy fur to gangly awkward teenagers within a few weeks.

Watching Rosie mature, physically and mentally, is truly a wonderful experience, and your personal interac-

should be high enough to keep the dog out of the mud and if you live in an area where snow or rain prevails, it's best to put some type of cover over the platform to help keep it dry. If in hot, dry country, a sunscreen is essential.

Rosie's doghouse can be constructed from wood or, if you prefer, commercial molded fiberglass doghouses are available in sizes to fit a Chessie. They are expensive, but should be a one-time investment. When shopping for a doghouse for a little puppy, it's sometimes difficult to remember that puppies grow up. Don't make the mistake of buying or building a house that will be too small for a full-grown Chessie. The dome-shaped, igloo types and the conventional rectangular fiberglass houses both have removable bottoms to facilitate cleaning. Some are also insulated, and are cooler in the summer and retain warmth in the winter.

There is one fact you must keep in mind; a kennel run provides the opportunity for limited exercise, but it doesn't provide the initiative to exercise. It gives your pet a certain amount of freedom, but it's your responsibility to see that Rosie gets the exercise she needs.

If Rosie sleeps in your home, elaborate outdoor housing is unnecessary. Keep in mind that if your yard fence is only 3 feet (1 m) tall, it can't contain an energetic and adventuresome adult Chessie. Such a fence is usually an adequate barrier when the family is with the dog, but if left alone behind a short fence, boredom or loneliness may stimulate Rosie to jump. Such a fence would be no challenge for a strong, athletic Chesapeake adult.

Crate Training

Owners often cringe at the thought of crating their Chessie, arguing that confinement of a large sporting dog in a crate is inhumane. If used properly,

Buy a crate large enough for an adult Chessie.

the crate is an excellent and harmless way to manage your puppy. It can also be used in certain cases when Rosie has reached adulthood, but you should never keep her in a crate for extended periods of time. Most dogs enjoy the cave-like atmosphere of a crate when sleeping, and a crate often makes a dog a welcome guest in motel rooms when you are traveling.

Obtain a large fiberglass crate with adequate ventilation. As in choosing a doghouse, don't make the mistake of buying a crate that is too small for an adult. Place some article of your clothing, the puppy's favorite toy, or a nylon bone in the crate together with a blanket or rug.

Lead Rosie into the crate, and quickly walk away. If she fusses or barks, respond with a sharp "No," and continue with your work. Confine Rosie to the crate for short periods of time in the beginning, but always leave the crate open when it isn't being used. Be sure to take her out of the crate frequently for eliminations.

Crating will soon be accepted and Rosie will have a "den" that she will

Cords of all types are attractive to pups.

use for naps or when the activity of the household becomes hectic or irritating. It will soon be one of her favorite places, one that is quiet and secluded.

When housebreaking Rosie, a crate is also handy. When so used, it should be partitioned off to fit the pup's size, so that the vacant space won't be used for a toilet. It may substitute for a wire pen or small room in which to confine her. It is also a great help when traveling, and is preferable to a seat belt to protect and control Rosie in your car.

A crate should never be used as a negative reinforcement in training. It should not be a means of punishment for doing something wrong. Give Rosie some special treat when she enters the crate and another when she is taken out. If you make crating a positive experience, she won't resent it.

Puppy-Proofing Your Home

Your puppy is ready for the house, but is your house ready for Rosie? Healthy puppies are rather destructive little creatures. Before she is left alone in your home for more than a few minutes, you should do a quick hazard inventory. Familiar objects that are

safe for the family may present some degree of danger to a new puppy. Look around for some of the following puppy hazards.

• Telephone or computer cords make wonderful tug-of-war toys for a pup. Unfortunately, the wires may not hold up very well against a Chessie attack and may be difficult to replace.

• Curtains or blinds that swing at Rosie's eye level are also quite challenging and may be attacked without provocation.

• Appliance and lamp cords are dangerous. If plugged in, they can cause mouth burns or fatal electrical shock when chewed. Those that are accessible to the puppy should be unplugged when Rosie is left unsupervised, even for a few minutes.

• A cord that is unplugged and visible is also attractive to a pup. Dangling cords attached to irons, toasters, radios, and other appliances are at risk.

• Oven cleaner, pesticides, and other poisonous household chemicals are sometimes accessible to an adventuresome pup. Laundry soap, bleach, dishwashing soap, silver cleaner, and other such products are frequently kept beneath the kitchen sink where they are an ever-present danger to puppies.

• Plastic pot-scrubbers and steel wool are notorious attractions for puppies. These as well as sponges may be chewed up and swallowed and may require surgical removal.

• If Rosie gets into a cupboard, try to ascertain what objects or chemicals may have been swallowed, read the labels, contact your veterinarian, and watch the pup carefully for signs of illness such as lethargy, vomiting, or diarrhea.

• Houseplants are another class of attractive targets for puppy attacks. Plant dangers are threefold. First, potted plants won't fight back and usually lose their lives. Second, a mixture of damp potting soil, shreds of leaves, stems, and roots are messy when spread over the carpet. Third, a few common house and garden plants are poisonous, and can cause serious illnesses in dogs.

• Silk flowers and other artificial foliage are not usually poisonous but they may upset Rosie's stomach, resulting in vomiting and diarrhea.

• Bookshelves that are within reach might appear to be a potpourri of leather and paper toys to Rosie.

• Children's rooms with the typical treasures are a wonderland of dangerous dog toys. Foam rubber balls, plastic toys, seashells, dolls, and other gimcracks and gewgaws are at risk. A small sponge rubber jacks ball may look harmless enough, but a Chessie puppy may swallow it without much effort, and unless it is retrieved quickly, it can require surgical removal. It's best to keep the doors to those rooms closed and off-limits to the pup.

• Tablecloths and coffee table scarves that hang over the tables' edges are great tug-of-war targets for a Chessie pup. Tasseled throw rugs also provide great fun and entertainment for mischievous Rosie.

Infant gates are inexpensive and easy to install to close off a room or two for Rosie. A portable dog pen that can be moved from room to room will serve the same purpose. These pens are available from any pet supply store and are much less expensive than the valuables they protect. Crating the pup is another way to control her actions when you can't watch her.

Puppy-proofing a house isn't easy; sometimes it's impossible. As an alternative plan, confine the young puppy to the yard or provide a safe, attractive play area in the garage.

A Chessie Puppy in Your Yard

You might think that a fenced yard is a perfect place for a pup, but when

Garden insect and fertilizer sprayers pose a health hazard to puppies.

Rosie gets bored, she may chew a wooden fence. If the fence doesn't extend into the ground several inches, she may decide to dig out.

Chemicals that have been recently applied to the lawn or garden should be watered well into the soil to prevent Rosie from contaminating her feet, then licking the toxins off. When watering the lawn after application of chemicals, be sure not to allow Rosie to drink from pools or puddles that form on sidewalks. Keep dogs off treated lawns for 48 hours!

In the garden shed are a number of other hazards. Puppy teeth can puncture garden hoses if they are not hung out of reach of the venturesome Chessie. Fertilizers and insecticides present major problems to pups, who may chew on a bag, box, or sprayer hose, and ingest toxic chemicals.

The danger of each product is plainly stated on the package labels. If your pup has possibly consumed any garden chemical, call your veterinarian immediately. Provide the label ingredients and the amount consumed, if it can be ascertained. Don't attempt to treat the puppy on your own unless you are unable to reach a professional.

Lonely pups get bored. Bored pups get into mischief.

In a backyard workshop, you will find more dangers. Paint removers are particularly dangerous, and even a quick investigative lick can cause severe tongue burns. A clumsy puppy might tip a can over, and soak her feet with the caustic stuff. In such an event, rinse her feet immediately with gallons of cool water. Then wash them off with soap and water and call your veterinarian. Keep paint, turpentine, thinner, and acetone well out of the dog's reach.

The Chessie loves to swim, but some backyard pools have escape ladders that are constructed for two-legged swimmers. If you have such a pool, provide a means of escape for your dog before she is allowed to come in contact with the pool. Show Rosie where the steps are, and teach her how to use them.

Chesapeake puppies aren't really animated, relentless, forces that are intent on self-destruction. The foregoing examples are worst case scenarios. All puppies are subject to mischievous activities that land them in trouble once in a while. By identifying hazards, you might save your puppy's life, or at least you may save yourself some money.

Exercise

A well-exercised pup is more apt to stay out of mischief and develop solid musculature and strong bones. Exercise aids in conditioning adults to keep them in prime hunting condition, and later will help minimize the effects of aging such as arthritis and obesity.

If you have a large fenced yard, Rosie will initiate some games by herself, but don't rely on self-imposed exercise to furnish her requirements. When children of the family romp and play with their Chessie friend, lack of exercise is rarely a problem. If Rosie is kept indoors or in a kennel run, you should help her exercise daily. Take

Keep in mind that the puppy is quite small and has a rapid metabolic rate. That makes the danger even greater and the need to get immediate professional help more demanding.

If Rosie has access to the garage, keep the floor and driveway clean and free from engine fluids that may drip from your car. Windshield washer fluid and other alcohol-containing products are equally dangerous. Virtually all automotive chemicals may be extremely hazardous to Rosie's health.

Antifreeze may contain a kidney toxin that can kill your dog. It has a sweet taste that attracts dogs, and, unfortunately, treatment is not very effective even when the poisoning is discovered early. Keep antifreeze out of reach of all pets. In the event that antifreeze poisoning is suspected, waste no time in obtaining professional help.

her to the lake to swim, initiate play sessions, take her jogging, or go on long walks. If your lifestyle doesn't allow you to spend time exercising your companion, consider a more sedentary pet.

Chewing

Chessie pups are happy, inquisitive characters with active mouths; like all puppies, they like to chew. The attraction to an item seems to be directly proportional to its replacement cost. A favorite child's toy or an expensive ski mitten will suffer the most abuse. For some unknown reason, old, worn-out shoes aren't as likely to be chewed as brand new ones. Shoes, regardless of their age or condition, should never be used as toys for a pup.

The potential for chewing shouldn't discourage you from obtaining a young pup, but it should warn you that your lifestyle will be affected by the presence of a new puppy. You should be prepared to pick up your personal belongings and stow them out of reach of the pup. Children should be taught to pick up their toys and clothes at the same time you are restricting Rosie to playing with her own toys.

A stern vocal reprimand should accompany each shoe-chewing episode. Immediately following the reprimand, you should offer Rosie some attractive and appropriate toy such as a nylon bone, knotted sock, or other chew toy. Refrain from giving her a rubber squeaker toy. The small metal squeaker is easily dislodged and can cause lots of digestive mischief if it is swallowed.

Automobiles

Fortunately, few dogs suffer any great fear of riding in cars. If the engine's noise or the vehicle's movement frightens Rosie, patience and short trips will gradually condition her to the engine noise and movement.

Boarding kennels should be booked well in advance.

When taking Rosie in the car, you decide where you want her to ride, and insist that she stay in the designated area. Dog safety harnesses are available in pet supply stores. The harness fastens into the automobile's seat belt system and holds her in a fairly confined area of the car. A crate is the safest and most positive means of confinement, but please don't put Rosie in a crate in the car's trunk!

Carsickness is accompanied by signs of abdominal distress such as nausea, salivation, and vomiting. If Rosie suffers from this malady, your veterinarian or the drugstore can provide motion sickness tablets. The dosage varies according to the size and age of the dog, and although most are relatively safe, you should check the product dosage with your veterinarian. In time, most dogs outgrow the problem, but until then, give a dose of the drug about an hour before your car trip. Rosie will appreciate it, and it beats cleaning up the mess afterward.

Avoid feeding your dog for two hours before an automobile trip. If

Rosie has a sensitive stomach, consider using a high-protein paste supplement as an energy substitute when traveling. Such products are available at most pet stores or veterinary offices, and provide temporary nutrition without the bulk of regular dog foods.

Those who drive a pickup truck are bound to consider allowing their Chessie to ride in the back. Fight the urge! If you insist, cross tie Rosie so it is impossible for her to leave the moving vehicle, and consult a veterinarian every few weeks about Rosie's eyes, which will no doubt suffer from the dust and debris flying about.

Boarding Kennels

Before you acquire your puppy, you should locate a place for her to stay when you can't be home. If you have a kennel run in your yard, find a neighbor or friend who will care for your pet there. That person should naturally make friends with Rosie before taking on the responsibility of her care. Don't allow her to stay in a backyard kennel for extended periods of time with no one to check on her food, water, and health.

An alternative might be to contact the person who raised your puppy. Some breeders have facilities to keep your dog for a time.

Commercial boarding kennels can present stress-related health risks to the dogs boarded therein. Settle on the least crowded and most secure boarding facility you can find. Family pets resent being enclosed in small areas; some become bored with inactivity and others are frightened or challenged by the commotion and barking of their kennelmates. Diet changes add to the stress of kenneled dogs. The odors of females in season are unnerving to intact males.

There are many excellent boarding kennels that are kept spotless and are well staffed and managed. Others may be a source of fleas, ticks, lice, and other external parasites. Inadequate cleaning may predispose boarders to intestinal parasite infestation. The most common complaint associated with commercial boarding kennels is kennel cough. This chronic, deep, croupy, honking cough may persist for weeks after your pet has returned home. (See Preventive Medicine, page 79.)

If boarding Rosie in a commercial kennel can't be avoided, visit the boarding facility before you need it and ask to tour the kennel. If a tour is denied, find another kennel. If you are allowed to walk through the kennel, watch for sick animals; signs of diarrhea, vomiting, coughing, and sneezing are indications that you are in the wrong kennel.

If possible, locate a kennel that specializes in boarding large dogs, one in which each dog has its own private indoor space that is connected to a large outdoor run. Look for runs that are separated from one another by block or brick walls instead of wire fencing. That arrangement will minimize conflict with neighbor dogs, and will also reduce exposure to respiratory infections.

Responsible boarding kennels require proof of a variety of inoculations prior to boarding your dog. Be pleased when you locate such a facility and be prepared to have Rosie's vaccination records available to be copied to their files. For a list of approved boarding kennels, see the American Boarding Kennel Association, page 99, in Useful Addresses and Literature.

Veterinary Care

Schedule a visit to your veterinarian when you acquire a new puppy, even if your Chessie is in perfect health. That professional will advise you of the appropriate timing of future booster vaccinations, as well as other preventive health measures that will protect Rosie's health.

New animal health ideas and products are introduced frequently in veterinary medicine. Research information may reveal better ways of immunizing dogs, treating or controlling parasites, preventing heartworm infestations, or detecting diseases.

Identification

Tattoos and Microchips

Even in the best-regulated households, puppies sometimes wander off. Rosie should be permanently identified as early as possible by tattooing or microchip implantation. Your veterinarian will advise you of the available means of identification and will help you implement your choice.

Routine vaccinations and physical exams are of vital importance for a new puppy.

No form of identification is effective however, unless you register Rosie with an animal relocation program. The AKC maintains a 24-hour hotline "Home Again" service. You can register Rosie's tattoo or microchip number with this service. The cost is minimal, and your veterinarian, pet supply store, or the AKC can provide you with a registration form. A veterinarian, humane society, shelter, or purebred rescue organization can scan for the microchip or look for a thigh or ear tattoo. It is up to the owner to keep the Home Again registry notified of changes in addresses or phone numbers.

Name Tags

Never allow Rosie outside without your name and address plainly visible on her collar. Identification tags are available through any pet supply store. Order one with your name, address and telephone number, and attach it securely to Rosie's collar. Buy a tag that rivets flatly to the web or leather collar. It will be furnished with the necessary rivets and no special application equipment is needed. If necessary, many shoe repairpersons will gladly rivet a tag flat against Rosie's collar for a modest fee. This type can't be easily lost and isn't apt to catch on branches or fences when the pup is playing. If nothing better is possible, print your name and telephone number in waterproof ink on the pup's nylon web collar.

If friends are watching your dog while you are on vacation, print their name and phone number in waterproof ink on a piece of gray duct tape and wrap it on Rosie's collar. Dogs are frequently lost when their owners are gone from home and cannot be reached by telephone.

Training Your Chesapeake

Housebreaking

"All training of the dog should be on the theory that he is a reasoning animal, possessing keen perception of cause and effect in connection with the circumstances which are within the scope of his animal needs, domestic life and every-day observation" (B. Waters 1895).

Learning may be associative, which means that the pup gets some reward for a particular desired action that is performed on command. Human socialization is also an example of associative learning. The pup learns

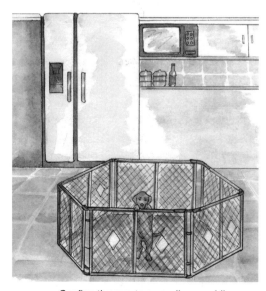

Confine the pup to a small area while housebreaking him.

while it is still quite young that handling and petting feel good. It learns that the human provides food and warmth. By associating these good feelings with the human, the dog becomes socialized. Learning can also be by habituation, which means that the dog becomes accustomed to a given incident. This type of learning includes training your Chessie to ignore gunshots by repeatedly exposing the dog to those noises. In any case, learning uses the intelligence of the dog to add to its natural traits.

To a pup, urinating isn't a mistake, it is natural. To housebreak Rowdy, you must impose human restrictions on his life. You must cause him to "think" like a human. He has no way of knowing about human customs until he is taught; therefore, you should never punish, scold, or reprimand him for messing on the floor. If you swat Rowdy when he is performing a natural act, you will confuse him. Rubbing his nose in his urine is equally confusing to the pup, and isn't likely to make a lasting impression on him. Once the act of urination or defecation is completed, it's gone from the puppy's mind.

Young puppies use little discretion, and when they feel the urge to urinate or defecate, they hardly hesitate a minute. The job is finished before you notice; then it's too late to correct. Dog trainers have estimated that to be effective, your response to a puppy's "accident" must occur within five seconds from the time it happens. After that time, the puppy will not associate its action with any corrective measure you may take.

For the first week or so, don't let Rowdy out of your sight when he is indoors. Each time he squats to urinate or defecate, say "*No*," in a normal tone of voice, pick him up, and carry him to the toilet area of the yard. Even if he has started to urinate or defecate, he should be carried outside to finish. Don't allow him to finish his job on the floor and then take him outside; that will only train Rowdy to take a trip to the backyard after each elimination.

After he has emptied his bladder or bowel in the toilet area, praise him and allow him back inside. Always take Rowdy to this special area of the yard for his eliminations. When the odors of previous eliminations are established in the toilet area, he will seek out that spot when necessary. Take him to that area immediately after each meal, when he wakes in the morning, after naps, and before bedtime at night. If you are able to train yourself to that task, he will be housebroken before you know it.

Prevention, substitution, and positive reinforcement are the most reliable tools to use in housebreaking your pup.
• Confine the pup. If you never let him out of your sight when he is indoors, you can *prevent* him from messing on the floor.
• When he shows signs of turning in circles in preparation for eliminating the bowel, pick him up quickly and *substitute* the toilet area of the yard for your carpet.
• When he complies and deposits his eliminations in the appropriate place, *praise and reward* him. To housebreak a pup, great patience is required, and persistence will pay off.

It isn't uncommon for a 12-week-old pup to learn to ring a bell to go

Puppies begin their training while still in the nest.

outside. You can hang a bell on the back door, take the pup to the door, ring the bell with his foot, and then open the door to allow him outside. Don't forget the reward when he performs correctly.

Until Rowdy is housebroken, pick up his food and water a couple of hours before bedtime and confine him in a crate or small pen during the night. If he fusses, you must take him to his toilet area. This is a fundamental concept of training; his fussing means a trip to the toilet. It doesn't mean attention, playtime, scolding, or food.

Don't expect miracles. After Rowdy is housebroken, he may still have an accident occasionally. That is not the time to lose your temper. His attention span is short but his memory is great. Once he fully understands what is expected of him, he will try to please you.

Paper Training

Paper training is rarely a long-term solution to any problem, and is only recommended in particular situations. If you find it necessary to paper train a pup, obtain a portable dog pen and confine the pup to the pen all the time when you aren't with him. Cover half the floor of the pen with layers of news-paper, and use the other half for the pup's food and water dishes, bed, and toys. The probability is that Rowdy will use the paper-covered area for elimina-tions right away. Always clean up his messes as soon as they are seen.

After a few days, the pen can be removed, leaving the papers in the same spot. When the pup is running free in the house and stops to urinate, rush him to the papers, and reward him when he uses them. Eventually, he will seek out and use the papers for his eliminations.

Collar and Leash Training

Collar and leash training is neces-sary for every dog, and the earlier you start the better. There are many meth-ods of training a dog to walk on a leash, but a positive approach should always be taken. Rowdy wants to fol-low you anyway, and all you must do is add first a collar, then a leash.

Your Chessie pup has never seen a collar and leash before, so you must have patience.

A nylon web buckle collar may be purchased for him at the pet supply store. Choke collars should always be used for training, but for elementary leash work in young puppies, a web collar is fine.

It should fit snugly, but not tight. When investing in a buckle collar for a young pup, buy one large enough to allow growth. For the first two or three days, the collar shouldn't be left on Rowdy when he is alone. After a few days of wearing his col-lar, he will tire of trying to scratch it off, and will ignore it. At that point, it is usually safe to leave the collar on him all the time.

As often as possible, snap a short leash on the collar and let Rowdy drag it around while you encourage him by offering a tidbit now and then. Once he is used to dragging the leash, pick it up and take a short walk around the yard. In the beginning, it's best to take only a few steps at a time, coaxing Rowdy to follow by offering tidbits from your fingers. The pup will soon con-nect the leash training with his rewards and he will welcome the appearance of his leash each day. Although it is important to let Rowdy know who has control of the leash, it should be done in a positive way, never roughly.

Pet supply stores have lightweight nylon leads of various strengths and lengths that retract into a plastic han-dle. These retracting leashes are con-venient and give Rowdy more freedom than standard leashes. They may be used after he has become accus-tomed to walking on a lead, but should not be used for training.

Once he has accepted the leash, you can exercise Rowdy out of his yard, and the new experiences, smells, and sights are ample reward for the restriction of the collar and leash. For a week or two, accustom him to the collar and leash and enjoy the companionship of your new pup.

From that easy beginning, you can gradually progress to teaching the pup to walk on your left side, in preparation for more advanced training. As Rowdy grows, the buckle collar should be replaced with a larger size, and it should be left on him all the time for identification.

Elementary Obedience Training

Natural Traits

All dogs will avoid soiling their living space if possible. Training a dog to use a toilet area is therefore simply expanding on his innate tendency to separate his residence from the site of his eliminations. A dog will instinctively follow a human who is kind to him, or come to someone who offers him a tidbit. We must remember that most of the things we train our dogs to do are not instinctive. A dog isn't born with the genetic desire to walk at heel, or to sit and stay. The dog trainer must overcome what is "natural" in order to cause that dog to honor certain human desires, such as walking on a leash, sitting, heeling, or staying. It is natural for a dog to enjoy tidbits, kind words, petting, and grooming. Therefore, by employing the principle of education with rewards, dogs can be taught to do amazing things. A willing dog, a dog that likes and trusts you, will obey and perform according to your commands and is easy to educate or train.

Some obedience training is necessary before you take Rowdy hunting or on walks around the neighborhood. This training, when approached gently, positively, and in short sessions, will be a rewarding experience. Obedience training may be started at any time, but shouldn't be pursued with vigor until Rowdy is about six months old. Prior to that time, the elements of each exercise may be introduced and practiced, but don't expect more than your pup's attention span is capable of producing.

When you begin obedience training, do it in privacy. Children or other onlookers pose a serious detriment to the training sessions. They will distract the dog, irritate the trainer, and generally slow the learning process. After Rowdy has mastered some of the work, you can show off what he knows.

Don't be discouraged when Rowdy becomes obstinate, sits down, drags his feet, and refuses to listen or cooperate. Have patience. The pup's attention span is short, and that which isn't learned today will be mastered tomorrow. Others have done this; certainly, you can do it too.

Hopefully, when you begin, the pup will have already accepted his leash. Remove the web collar and put a choke collar in its place, snap on a sturdy nylon web leash, and begin the first exercise.

Choke Collar

This piece of equipment is misnamed; it doesn't "choke" the dog if used correctly. A choke collar should always be used for training. It is formed from a short piece of smooth chain or strong nylon cord with a ring

A chain or nylon "choke collar" must be placed on the dog correctly to be effective and safe.

attached to each end. In order to work properly, it must be fitted to the dog. It should measure approximately 2 inches (5 cm) greater than the circumference of the dog's neck.

To form the collar, drop the chain (or cord) through one of the rings to form a noose, and snap the leash into the free ring. Place the collar on Rowdy so the end of the collar that is attached to the leash comes up his left side and crosses from left to right over the top of his neck. Rowdy is maintained on your left side, and when it is necessary to correct the dog's action, the collar is given a quick tug, then released. If a choke collar is placed on the dog's neck incorrectly, it will not release quickly, and may injure the dog. A choke collar that is too long will not close quickly enough to be effective. Keep in mind that the foregoing discussion assumes that the dog will be walking on your left side.

Pronged Collars

Training collars are available that are made of a dozen or so hinged wire prongs. The dull prongs turn against the dog's neck when the leash is tightened. They may be an effective way of training an obstreperous dog, but are rarely needed on a Chessie. They should be used only by professional trainers (if necessary), and when used, must never be abused. If you think you need a pronged collar to control your Chessie, have a professional teach you the proper usage of this device. Prong collars are banned from the premises of AKC shows.

Electronic training collars are preferable to prong collars but should also be used with discretion. Watch a professional trainer use one and be sure you understand just how and why these devices are meant to be used before you invest in one. The shock from an electronic collar is not sufficient to burn or seriously hurt the dog if used properly.

Command Clarity

If this is your first dog training attempt, remember it's also Rowdy's first training and you both need patience if you are to succeed. This is a partnership effort—cooperation and understanding are essential on both ends of the leash.

Divide each command into five parts, and make each part clear and distinct. Rowdy has better hearing than you do, so shouting isn't going to add anything positive to the training. The command shouldn't be repeated time and again for a single function.

First, say the dog's *name* clearly. This is difficult when his name is complex or lengthy, so if necessary, shorten the name and make it a simple two-syllable word. When you say "*Rowdy*," you'll get his attention; that lets him know that you will soon give a command that you expect to be followed. After a delay of a second or two, give the *command*. After another few seconds, *enforce* the action, gently and firmly. After the action has been successfully performed, *release* him from the command and offer a *reward* with your praise.

It is best to schedule training sessions before mealtimes and use small treats to encourage the pup. Patience, privacy, and positive reinforcement will win out.

Come

Always begin training with a simple, easily understood command. You will probably teach your pup to come at feeding time, without either of you realizing what you are doing. It is one exercise that can be learned by a young pup, and the sooner it is mastered the better.

Fasten a 20-foot (6-m) lightweight nylon line to Rowdy's collar. Allow him to wander away from you for some distance. Then drop to one knee and give the command, "*Rowdy* (hesitation)

Obstinate, who's obstinate?

come." If Rowdy doesn't respond with the enthusiasm you desire, give a tug or two on the line, repeating the command crisply. When Rowdy arrives on your lap, lavish praise on him and give him a tidbit. Then release him from the exercise with an "*OK*," and continue to praise him. Allow him to wander off again, and repeat the exercise.

When his response to the command has become automatic, try him off leash, in the fenced yard. Use the

Enforce the sit *command by gently pushing your Chessie's bottom to the ground.*

command several times daily for grooming, feeding, and especially for petting, but never call your dog to you to scold or discipline him. That will defeat your purpose. Instead, each time he comes on command, praise and pet him, regardless of what mischief you have called him away from.

Sit

With your puppy standing on your left side, in a calm, normal voice, say "*Rowdy*." Wait a second before you say "*Sit*," and when that command has been absorbed, push the pup's bottom to the ground. It's important to allow a few seconds after the *sit* command is given before helping him to sit. This hesitation allows time for him to understand exactly what you desire. Rowdy must associate the command with the desired action. As you enforce the *sit* command, offer a tidbit to Rowdy at his eye level, immediately in front of and very close to his muzzle. This will encourage him to sit and stay in that position. After a few sec-

onds of sitting, release him by saying, "*OK*," then praise him. A food reward need only be used in the beginning, but praise and petting must be given in abundance after each exercise is performed correctly.

Practice the sitting exercise several times a day, but don't expect miracles! If you're lucky, the dog will catch on the first day, but don't count on it. Don't add to his confusion with more training at this time.

When Rowdy makes a mistake, use the word "*Wrong*," in a conversational tone, before you make the correction. Reserve "*No*," in a gruff voice, for times when Rowdy is in trouble, and you want him to refrain altogether from whatever mischief he is involved in.

In the next session, practice the *come* and *sit* commands several times, and if met with success, progress to another exercise. After the fundamentals of training are absorbed, Rowdy will listen for the command, and will respond to new commands more readily. Some dogs take longer to catch on than others and ten-week-old puppies aren't usually as quick to learn simple exercises as older dogs.

Stay

When Rowdy has mastered sitting, and is looking for his tidbit, tell him "*Stay*" while you remain standing at his right side. Present your outstretched palm in front of his muzzle as you give the command "*Stay*." If he tries to lie down or stand up, tell him "*Wrong*," repeat the command "*Stay*," and put him back into a sitting position. After a few seconds, release him from the stay with an "*OK*," and give him a reward.

Be consistent; always break the command into several parts: his name, the command "*Sit, Stay*," enforcement of the action, the release, and finally the reward and praise.

After Rowdy has absorbed the *stay* command, move away from him while he is in the *sit-stay* position. The first few times you put the leash on the ground and start to walk away, he will try to follow. Say "*Wrong*," repeat the command "*Stay*," place him in the sitting position, display your outstretched flat palm, and back away again. After a few tries, the pup will get the idea and stay put while you take several steps backward, then return to finish the exercise. Always release him from the stay, and when the exercise is finished, give him praise and reward.

He won't understand what you are asking him to do at first. Take only a few steps backward in the beginning. Return quickly to his side, take your position with Rowdy on your left, pick up the leash, and release him from the *stay* command. Most pups do well if they stay for 20 seconds without fidgeting.

Fold the pup's forelegs and push his body to the ground as you give the down *command.*

a few steps. Finish the exercise by returning to him, releasing him from the exercise, and lauding great praise upon him. Once the pup realizes that you aren't leaving him, and if he stays you will return with more praise, he will be happy to cooperate.

Down

This obedience command is a convenient way to let the pup relax while you talk to neighbors on your daily walks. It is given in the same way that the *sit* command is used. Begin the exercise with the dog in the sitting or standing position. The command is "*Rowdy* (hesitation), *down.*" Don't muddy the command with extra words. If you tell him "*Rowdy, lie down*" or "*Rowdy, sit down,*" it is bound to confuse him. Be consistent; always use the same words.

After you have given the *down* command, exert pressure on his back, pushing his body to the ground, slowly and gently. Don't fight him. If necessary, hold a tidbit so low that he can't reach it without lying down. Or if he doesn't cooperate, push him to the sitting position, and fold his elbows, placing his belly against the ground.

When he has mastered the *down* command, add "*Stay*," and back away

Heel

Rowdy is now familiar with his leash, and doesn't panic when you

Heeling is boring to the dog, and shouldn't be continued for extended periods.

47

Chessies are anxious to please.

occasionally tug on it. Each time you bring it out, Rowdy realizes that a walk is on the morning's agenda and new vistas are about to be discovered.

Heeling is a more advanced exercise that all well-behaved dogs should learn before they are taken into busy, crowded situations. Place Rowdy on your left side, run the leash through your left hand and hold it with your right. Begin with the command, "*Rowdy, sit.*" Then as you step off with your left foot, give the command "*Heel.*" Walk straight ahead, keeping him beside your left leg with gentle tugs on the leash as necessary.

If he is accustomed to running ahead of you, you must hold him back by controlling the short leash or by changing direction. When Rowdy is anxious to investigate something at the far end of his leash, keep it short, but don't hold the leash too tightly.

Leave slack enough for him to move a step ahead or behind you, but don't allow him to bolt ahead. When you correct him, don't jerk him off balance; instead, if he moves past your left knee, do an about-face and walk in the opposite direction. Say "*Rowdy, heel*" as you make that turn. Soon he will pay attention; he will watch where you put your left foot and keep his body in line with you.

After he has properly "heeled" for a dozen steps, stop, and push his bottom to the ground to the sitting position as you give the command "*Sit.*" Then release him with an "*OK,*" reward him with a tidbit and praise, and begin the exercise all over again. If the pup wants to lag behind, encourage him to keep up with you by teasing him along with a tidbit held in your right hand. Soon your Chessie will be walking by your side, taking turns and stops in his stride. If he refuses to walk at your side, stop the exercise and wait a week before your resume. Don't forget to keep the training exercises short, no more than five minutes each, with a playtime between exercises.

Teaching a dog to heel is an excellent discipline exercise; it is a must for dog shows, or when you are walking in a crowd on a busy street, but that's where heeling should end. It is the most boring exercise Rowdy will learn. He should be given more freedom whenever the situation and space will allow.

After he has mastered heeling, when going for a walk, a retracting flexible lead may be substituted for his short leash to allow Rowdy more freedom to investigate. Soon, your pup will recognize his various equipages and connect each to the type of work or play that you have in mind. When he sees his choke collar, he will know that you intend to maintain maximum control. Obedience work is anticipated. If you leave his web collar on, and pick up the short leash, that will tell him that this is to be a fun time or a controlled walk. And if he spots his retractable leash and web collar, it means a romp in the park.

Repeat the training that you have started every day or if that isn't possible, at least several times a week. A puppy's attention span is very limited. In order to fix the learned behavior in his mind and make it automatic, training must be continued and repeated.

All pups are active, inquisitive, mischievous and energetic; they misbehave sometimes. They aren't automatons; they are intelligent beings that are anxious to learn and to please you. Don't make a federal case out of each mistake Rowdy makes. He likes to play and have fun, and as a teacher, you should always try to make his education as painless as possible. No single training exercise session should take more than a few minutes. If continued overly long, Rowdy will lose interest. Change frequently from one exercise to another, and don't forget to play with the pup between exercises.

Don't expect the pup to be ready for an obedience ring at the end of the first week of training.

Negative Reinforcement

"The common belief seems to be that the dog acts from the impulse of instinct throughout his life. Many people concede no higher mentality to him than what comes from instinct, and this too notwithstanding that true instincts are independent of experience; while the dog's knowledge is dependent on experience and education. A few people proceed on the theory that punishment will force a knowledge into the dog's consciousness" (B. Waters 1895).

Don't use negative reinforcement when attempting to educate your dog. It is a mistake to spank or scold a pup that is guilty of nothing more than bouncing up when he should be sitting. The Chessie has a phenomenal memory; he will remember the spanking, but he might never understand what action on his part precipitated the punishment.

Feeding Your Chesapeake

A Chessie's physical and mental condition, performance, longevity, general health, and energy are directly related to the food she eats. Any discussion of canine nutrition must begin with one simple fact. If something is advertised that looks too good to be true, it probably is. A dollar's worth of nutrition can't be packaged to sell for a few cents. Rosie is a valuable resource, and dog food quality is a poor place to economize.

Dry dog food should be kept in airtight containers. It is less expensive in 50-pound (22.7-kg) bags, but storage can take its toll on nutrients when the

Give careful thought to your selection of dog food by basing your choice on the best nutrition, not the lowest price.

food is exposed to the air. Fats may become rancid; vitamins A, D, E, K, and some B complex may be lost. For that same reason, beware of buying dry dog food from stores that have low product inventory turnover, and don't buy excessive quantities at one time.

A few dry dog foods are preserved with natural antioxidants such as vitamins C and E, and contain no artificial preservatives. Such foods may or may not prove to be better sources of nutrition than those containing preservatives and additives to help maintain their palatability and to protect them from early oxidation. Don't store bagged dog food in warm places because elevated temperatures enhance deterioration of the ingredients.

Excellent premium foods are available in pet supply stores and supermarkets and from veterinarians. Nutritional information on these packages will specify whether the product provides optimum nutrients for growth in puppies, reproduction, working dogs, or adult maintenance.

Types of Foods

Canned Foods

Of the three types of dog foods that are presently on the market, canned foods are usually the most expensive, but they store well and are highly palatable. Feeding canned food alone may not give Rosie an adequate amount of roughage in her diet and may predispose her to urinary frequency. Canned food is over 60 percent water, and has preservatives that may cause a diuretic effect when canned food is fed exclusively. The meat contained in canned dog foods often isn't of the highest quality in spite of what dog food commercials would have you believe.

Semimoist

Palatability and appearance are the principal selling points of soft-moist or semimoist foods, but they don't store as well as canned foods. They have the appearance of hamburger or ground meat, but if you read the labels, you might be surprised what ingredients are in the product. They are expensive and contain rather large amounts of sugar and some question-able chemical preservatives that are not found in dry foods.

Feeding semimoist foods often leads to high water consumption that results in frequent urination. Semimoist foods are also often incriminated as the cause for certain allergic reactions.

Dry Foods

The least expensive diet for Rosie is a dry dog food. These foods can be fed exclusively, but they aren't all the same; they vary greatly in nutritional content and palatability. It shouldn't be necessary to flavor Rosie's food or to add supplements to a dry dog food to make it a complete and balanced diet.

Varieties of Dry Food

There are three general varieties of dry dog foods: premium, commercial, and generic.

Premium Brands

Premium brands are usually the most expensive dry dog foods on the market, and yet they are often the most economical. They are sold in vet-erinary hospitals, pet supermarkets, and, occasionally, grocery stores. They are usually quite palatable and well

Look for an AAFCO feeding trial declaration on the label of your dog food.

accepted by dogs. Generally, premium dry dog foods contain adequate nutri-tion and require no supplementation. In many cases, these foods may be offered free choice, meaning that the food is left out so the dog has access to it at all times, to be eaten whenever desired. Naturally that is not an option if your Chessie is a glutton.

To increase palatability, a basic diet of complete and balanced dry food may be mixed with premium canned food of the same quality.

Commercial Brands

Commercial foods are those that are found stacked on the shelves of grocery stores, supermarkets, and dis-count stores. Many of them provide excellent nutrition, and some of the name brands have found a place in the market for decades. Any discus-sion of these commercial foods is rela-tive, because they vary in number and

51

Good nutrition is important for the brood bitch and her pups.

tional elements will proudly display that information.

Study dog food labels and call or write to manufacturers. Know what you are feeding Rosie! Buying a dog food that is cheaper than others, or because the total protein is higher than other brands, makes no more sense than choosing a food by the picture on a bag. The *sources* and *quality* of protein, carbohydrate, and fat are as important as the quantities.

Don't fall prey to "cute" television ads that typically show a beautiful litter of puppies, a happy companion dog, or a group of "winning dogs." Those paid actors are marketing tools and they may or may not be promoting a superior dog food.

If a label states that the dog food meets the recommendations of the National Research Council (NRC), it may apply only to canine *maintenance* requirements, and the food should be adequate for pets that are under minimal stress. Those foods may not be acceptable for growing puppies, performance dogs, or breeding animals, because they don't supply the increased energy demands of work, training, growth, pregnancy, or lactation.

Labels often specify the quantities of available nutrients, not the *bioavailable* nutrients (the amount of the food that can actually be used by the dog for its energy requirements). If an essential element is fed to a dog in a form that is not bioavailable, it might as well be left on the store shelf.

The ingredient list should give you the source of protein contained in the food. Protein of vegetable origin such as wheat, corn, or soy flour may provide an excellent analysis on the package, but it may be misleading if that protein is not bioavailable.

quality. As a general rule, you might wish to contact the manufacturer and ask for the data on the food being considered. You should receive a report on any feeding trials being conducted, the sources of all the ingredients, and the analysis.

Generic Brands

Generic brands should always be considered, but before buying, be sure they conform to the standards discussed in the following paragraphs. Generic foods may vary in composition from month to month, as various grains or other ingredients become more or less available. Rarely will generic foods be proven in feeding trials, due to the expense of those trials.

If you decide to use generic foods, ask the department manager which food turns over the quickest, read the label, check the ingredients, and make your purchase.

Dog Food Labels

All products should list their composition; if they don't, pick another product. Dog foods containing the best ingredients and balanced nutri-

Feeding Trials

Some foods, usually the premium brands, will include the label declara-

A well-balanced diet is essential for solid bone growth.

tion that the food has passed the American Association of Feed Control Officials (AAFCO) feeding trials for the entire life cycle of canines. These products should contain the right amount of bioavailable food elements required for puppies, youths, and working adults.

If the AAFCO declaration is not shown, it doesn't necessarily mean that the food hasn't been subjected to feeding trials. Call the manufacturer and ask to see the feeding trial results, and ask about the sources of protein and fat. Ask if the formula is kept constant, regardless of the seasonal variation of ingredient costs.

When the desired information about a product is not available, choose another brand. If you are unable to understand the information provided by manufacturers, consult with your veterinarian. If he or she isn't able to help you make the decision, borrow a text on the subject. Most veterinary clinics have reference sources for nutritional requirements of dogs.

Nutritional Elements

Water
Fresh drinking water must be supplied for Rosie all her life. Other nutritional elements may be varied under different circumstances, but a source of clean water is always essential. That doesn't mean adding water to a dirty pan. Dogs, like humans, prefer cool, fresh water in a clean receptacle.

Protein
Amino acids (protein components) from vegetables have less bioavailability than those from animal proteins. The dog is a carnivore, a meat eater. Relative to optimum canine nutrition, plant protein is of lower quality than animal protein.

Fats
Adequate fat must be included in your Chesapeake's diet. Fat is a calorie-dense nutrient that contains 9 Kcal (the amount of heat energy required to

Be sure your pup has fresh, clean water at least once daily or more often during hot weather.

raise 1 kg of water from 15 to 16°C) per gram. That is more than twice the calories of protein and carbohydrates. This is true of both animal fat and vegetable oil. Palatability is the principal difference between vegetable and animal fats. Both provide adequate fatty acids.

Carbohydrates

Carbohydrates (starches) are also sources of calories that are derived from plants. In human diets, they are important sources of glucose, but the canine requirement for carbohydrates is not significant. Although dogs don't require starches, it is impractical to produce dog foods without them. Dog foods that are high in plant carbohydrates and contain protein and fat that are also of plant origin are not recommended. A food that combines animal protein with plant carbohydrates and fats is the best nutrition for a dog.

Vitamin Supplements

A balanced diet, such as a premium food, needs no vitamin or mineral supplementation. It is a mistake to feed a bargain brand of dog food and hope to cover its inadequacies with a cheap vitamin-mineral supplement. Supplements can be dangerous; check with your veterinarian before feeding them to your Chessie.

The bioavailability and protein quality found in dog foods of the past were often suspect, and nutritionists recommended adding bonemeal and meat, especially liver, to them. Recent research by pet food manufacturers, private research foundations, and universities have revealed a world of information about the nutritional needs of our pets. Complete and balanced diets have been formulated for us.

Influence of Nutrition on Coat Quality

Rowdy's coat quality is a reflection of his nutritional status and general condition. To maintain a beautiful coat will require more than brushing or combing it once in a while. If he is maintained on a premium dog food and is exercised often, his coat will probably always look great. Nutrition involves more than just what you feed him.

Internal parasites rob the dog of nutrition, and are thus associated with dietary insufficiencies and a poor coat. A roundworm infestation influences the appearance of a dog's coat, as does a hookworm problem. Hookworms cause blood loss and may contribute to general ill health that is manifested by coat problems and anemia.

External parasites such as fleas or lice rob the dog of nutrition regardless of its diet. They cause many vague physical and mental signs in the dog and contribute to poor coat condition.

Pregnancy, whelping, and lactation are significant stressors on a brood bitch's system, and will always cause the bitch to lose coat and appear ratty for several weeks. These stresses are partially nutritional in origin.

As your dog ages, his ability to absorb certain nutrients is impaired; his nutritional needs change and if those needs aren't met, he may display coat problems.

Sometimes dietary supplements are used to help "dress up" the coat. Such coat conditioners are an unnecessary expense, but they may be advised after the nutritional cause of the poor coat is treated. The best way to attain a shiny coat with rich colors is through good nutrition, not from a bottle of coat enhancer. Check with your veterinarian before you use lecithin, vitamin A, corn oil, or other coat-enhancing preparations.

Readers who wish to learn more about canine nutrition can purchase the book *Nutritional Requirements of Dogs, Revised*, from the National Research Council, telephone 1-800-624-6242. That inexpensive volume is updated regularly and will answer virtually all of your technical questions about canine nutrition.

Homemade Diets

The family kitchen is usually a poor place to formulate your dog's food. Homemade diets often lead to problems, and you are advised to leave dog food production to those who have laboratories, research facilities, and feeding trials to prove their products.

Frequency of Feeding

When your seven-week old puppy arrives in your home, she should be fed free choice dry puppy food, plus two moist meals of canned and dry food daily. Gradually increase the quantity of these moist meals as she grows. This schedule should be continued until Rosie is six months of age. From six months until a year of age, one moist meal per day is fed, together with the free choice dry food. After a year of age, most dogs will do quite nicely on free choice dry food exclusively.

This free choice schedule can't be followed if Rosie turns out to be a gluttonous eater, or if you have other dogs that are overeaters.

If free choice feeding isn't a viable option for your dog(s), feed Rosie three times daily while a puppy and twice daily when she is six months to a year old. During hunting season, heavy training, or anytime that Rosie is working hard, she needs more nutrition than her maintenance allowance. The best way to determine nutritional need is to weigh her weekly. If she is losing weight, increase her diet; if she is gaining, reduce it.

Dietary No-No's

Milk will usually bring on a bout of diarrhea, as will organ meat (liver, heart, kidney), rich foods, and table scraps. Avoid feeding these items. They may also serve to upset your Chessie's stomach and interfere with her nutrition. Cooked bones are yet another attractive nuisance for the dog. Chicken or chop bones, steak bones, ribs, and some roast bones may splinter when Rosie chomps down on them. Bone shards may lodge in the dog's mouth or throat or they may be swallowed where they can cause other mischief. Ice cream, candy, pizza, potato chips, and a host of other human junk foods are difficult for the dog to digest and should also be avoided. Stay away from chocolate; it can poison the dog.

Inappropriate Eating Habits

If Rosie is a glutton and tends to be fat, you must take the responsibility of feeding her meals that won't perpetuate her gluttonous habits. If she is housed with another dog, it will be necessary to separate them at mealtime. Measured amounts should be fed, and the dog's weight and condition should be monitored frequently.

Good nutrition produces great dogs.

Obesity may also be treated in a young dog by adding low-calorie fillers to her diet. Ground carrots, canned green beans, or other low-calorie foods may be added to her balanced diet without upsetting it appreciably.

Older dogs that are obese may just be lazy, and when a dog begins to age and no longer exercises for hours each day, her food must be cut back. It is important to reevaluate her nutritional needs when you begin the cut-back program, because nutritional requirements change with age. In a healthy dog, a higher quality food in reduced quantity will usually control an old dog's obesity.

Sudden weight gain accompanied by a voracious appetite is cause for alarm. A number of health problems, including diabetes, may cause weight gain.

If Rosie remains skinny, but is full of energy, don't despair. Some Chessies are so ambitious and energetic that they remain thin all their lives. They burn all the calories that their diets furnish, and store none. It is best to feed such dogs premium foods—free choice or frequent small meals of dry food mixed with canned food each day. If a continued weight loss or loss of energy is seen in a thin dog, if her coat becomes dry, or if any other signs of ill health appear, a veterinary examination is needed.

Grooming Your Chessie

Your Chessie's coat may glisten with a natural sheen, but that doesn't relieve you of grooming responsibilities. Brushing, combing and occasional bathing is a necessary part of dog ownership. Grooming sessions should be scheduled, and shouldn't be allotted to your "spare time." Another mistake is to assign grooming duties to an unsupervised youngster.

When to Groom

This important part of Rowdy's bonding and training should begin shortly after you acquire the pup. Grooming Rowdy will establish trust and obedience and it may be done daily if your schedule allows. It isn't necessary to spend more than a few minutes at the task; frequency is more important than duration. The procedure is beneficial in several other ways. The puppy is taught to stand or sit still on the table while you groom him. Daily examination of Rowdy's feet, pads, and ears accustoms him to handling, and he is less likely to resist having his entire body touched as he matures.

Establish a routine for grooming; place him on a table or countertop if possible. If you hold the pup on your lap while grooming him, you will encourage him to chew, try to play, or escape. Let him know that grooming is serious business; don't let Rowdy jump from the table while you are combing him. Be sure he understands the necessity and certainty of the procedure. A pup bonds to the person who disciplines and trains him and with whom he spends the most time. He respects the person who handles him the most, and by regular grooming, you are establishing yourself as his leader.

As an adult, when Rowdy is exercised in the country, or is hunting, grooming should be a routine procedure that follows every run in the field. You can find and remove thistles and cheat-grass awns from between his toes and those that are caught in his ears. Footpad injuries can be discovered and medicated, as well as eye irritations that result from running in dense brush or swimming.

While grooming, you may discover minor health problems, such as a broken tooth, an early ear infection, fleas, or ticks. When these problems are recognized early, the treatment is far less extensive and less costly than if allowed to progress.

A well-groomed Chessie.

57

HOW-TO:
Groom Your Chesapeake

Brushing and combing should be done routinely, but only bathe Rowdy if his coat is deeply soiled or fouled, or shortly before a dog show. If Rowdy encounters a skunk, or finds something rancid to roll in along the hiking trail, it is usually time for a bath. A bath will also help finalize his seasonal shedding. Pick a warm day, or plan to spend half an hour in the house with him. Prepare the following equipment:
- Stainless steel comb with wide-set teeth
- Flea comb
- Pin brush with short, wire bristles
- Scissors-type nail trimmer
- Styptic shaving stick
- Electric hair dryer with warm setting
- Bathtub with hair-collecting drain stopper)
- Sprayer hose connected to a faucet
- Mild dog shampoo without insecticides
- Stack of dry towels
- Cotton balls
- Rubbing alcohol

Combing

Comb and brush all of the loose hair from Rowdy's coat to get the dead hair off the dog and into the brush instead of on the furniture and carpet. Don't be cross if he is impatient and anxious for you to finish, and reward him by playing for a while when finished. When combing his coat, pay particular

Make thin, serial slices of the dark nails to be sure you don't get one too short.

attention to the top of the pelvic area, immediately in front of his tail; run the fine-tooth flea comb through the hair of this area. If fleas are present, they will hop out ahead of the comb or will be caught in the teeth of the comb.

Nail Care

When needed, trim Rowdy's nails with a sharp nail trimmer of the scissors type. Long, pointed puppy nails often need attention weekly. Chessies that live outside may not require the nails of their forefeet to be trimmed nearly as often. They require trimming only when they begin to grow downward and peck on the tile floor. Old dogs' nails should be checked more frequently. Front nails usually demand less attention than hind nails, which often need trimming on a regular basis. Nail trimming sometimes requires two sets of hands and a firm conviction on the owner's part. If you begin this routine when Rowdy is a small puppy, it will be better accepted all his life.

Perhaps one or two of Rowdy's nails are sufficiently transparent to see the blood vessels forming a point in the core or quick of the nail. You can use the beam of a penlight to identify the quick. Your first cut should be just beyond that forward pointing, V-shaped vascular structure. By visually measuring the length of the light nail after trimming it, you should have a good idea about how much to take off the darker nails.

When in doubt or if all nails are dark, begin cutting off thin

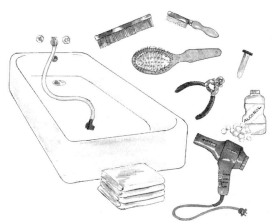

Proper grooming equipment is important.

58

serial slices of the nail, starting at the tip. As the slices near the quick, the nail becomes softer with each slice. Your first slices near the tip of the nails will have cross sections that are hollow at the bottom, forming an inverted V-shape. As you near the blood vessels in the quick, the slices will become more nearly circular when viewed in cross sections.

An electric rotary hand tool with a sandpaper drum can also be used to shorten and sand off rough edges from toenails. They grind very quickly however, and you must be careful not to grind too deep.

Slight bleeding of a too-short nail shouldn't be cause for alarm; it isn't likely to be profuse, but it may be persistent. A few drops of blood look like a quart when spread over a white tile floor. To stop the bleeding, press a dampened styptic shaving stick firmly to the bleeding nail. Hold it in place for several minutes, and keep the dog confined to his crate for an hour after the bleeding has stopped.

Ears

After each excursion to the field, or trip to the lake, examine Rowdy's ears. Ear cleaning is an important part of regular grooming in hunting dogs. Wax or dirt deposits in the outer ear canal can easily be cleaned with a cotton ball moistened with alcohol. Don't pour any cleaning solution into Rowdy's ears unless advised by your veterinarian. Be aware of unusual sensitivity, and if he scratches at either or both ears, or holds his head tipped to the side when you touch one,

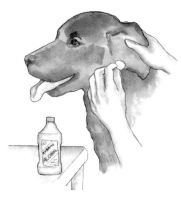

Wipe excess wax from the outer ear canal with cotton balls moistened with alcohol.

have the ears examined before initiating any treatment. Cheat-grass awns or wild oat seeds are commonly found in the outer ear canals of field dogs, and may lead to serious infections. (See Grass Awns, page 81.)

Eyes

Rowdy's eyes should be inspected after field trips or

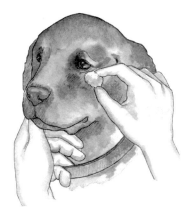

Careful examination of the eyes is especially important after your Chessie has been out hunting or running in the field.

swimming and when he is groomed. Look for redness, irritation, and foreign material. Field dogs often collect grass seeds or minute plant particles under one of their eyelids. If Rowdy squints, he may have a grass seed under his eyelid. This usually requires a trip to the veterinarian to remove the foreign material before it has rubbed on the cornea.

Bathing

If bathing is necessary, place Rowdy in the bathtub and soak his coat thoroughly with warm water, using a spray nozzle that is held close to his skin. Use a mild dog shampoo sparingly and work it into a copious lather. Keep the soap well away from his face and eyes, and don't squirt water into his ears. When the entire coat has been lathered, rinse it out with the spray nozzle, going over the coat several times, until all shampoo is gone.

Towel Rowdy several times, rubbing his coat vigorously and changing towels frequently, to squeeze as much water as possible from the coat. Take him out of the bathtub and using the warm setting on the dryer, complete the drying procedure. That part is unnecessary if you have chosen a warm summer day.

You shouldn't bathe your water retriever thoroughly for at least a month before duck hunting season. Bathing will partially remove some of the natural oils that protect his coat and skin from the ice and cold water—one of the reasons why a Chesapeake is such a great swimmer.

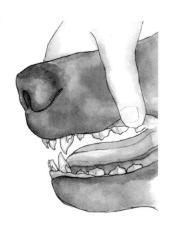

Double teeth sometimes require a veterinarian's attention.

Calluses

While grooming, watch for abnormalities that may be present on the skin. Callus formation usually begins on the outside of a dog's elbows, and later they may form on the hocks, sides of the feet, and hipbones. They are rarely a problem in pets but they are common in kenneled dogs that are kept on concrete or wooden floors. Calluses aren't generally a serious health problem unless they become infected, but they are unsightly. If the calluses are hard, cracked, or infected, consult your veterinarian.

Lanolin and vitamin E applications may be applied to early callus formations to keep them soft and pliable. Calluses may be of considerable concern in your Chessie after the age of six or seven.

Teeth

Rowdy may develop two sets of teeth between three and six months of age. It is common for a dog's permanent teeth to emerge through the gums before the deciduous (tempo-rary) teeth are lost. If his baby teeth are loose and wriggly, no treatment is necessary. If the permanent teeth have reached full growth and the baby teeth are still anchored solidly in the gums, those deciduous teeth should be extracted. Don't attempt extraction at home. A pair of pliers might break the teeth off and make Rowdy mad, and you will still have the expense of a trip to the animal hospital.

Solid baby teeth that are situated alongside the permanent teeth may interfere with the normal alignment of the adult teeth. If they aren't impinging on the adult teeth, the tight space between the two sets of teeth often collects hair and debris that contribute to halitosis (bad breath) and gingivitis (gum infection).

If Rowdy is given rawhide or nylon bones to chew, and is on a dry food diet, his teeth shouldn't require much routine care.

Note: Most dogs enjoy the taste of harmless-appearing rawhide bones and other rawhide chewies and they present no problem. There have been some reports of dogs swallowing large pieces of these chew sticks, which are not readily digested and remain intact in the stomach, causing no end of grief. Give them to your dog advisedly and watch for digestive problems.

Dogs rarely develop dental cavities unless the teeth are broken. Older dogs, and those that don't chew a lot, often develop tartar deposits. As this plaque builds up, it invades and erodes the gums and promotes bacterial infections (gingivitis). If allowed to progress unchecked, this infection will cause the teeth to loosen. Chronic gingivitis may predispose older dogs to arthritis or heart and kidney disease.

If yellow tartar is seen, try cleaning the teeth with gauze pads moistened with hydrogen peroxide. Peroxide will help control gingivitis, and often will dissolve the soft, early dental tartar.

Ethel, the picture of a happy Chessie.

Pet supply stores or your veterinarian will supply you with canine toothpaste and toothbrushes, and brushing Rowdy's teeth can be worked into his regular grooming schedule. Adult dogs often resent having their teeth brushed, but if you begin while he is still a puppy, Rowdy will become accustomed to it and accept this oral hygiene process. If tartar builds up in spite of your efforts, your veterinarian can scale the teeth with ultrasonic equipment and dental instruments. Sometimes that procedure requires a short-acting general anesthetic.

Work for Your Chesapeake

The Versatile Chesapeake

Several AKC breeds are called "dual-purpose" dogs to indicate that they are exhibited in conformation shows as well as field trial competitions. The Chesapeake is one of those dogs, although it is a breed that hasn't received much recognition as a dual-purpose dog.

An intelligent and biddable Chessie often also does well in obedience trials, and with specialized training Chessies excel in retriever trials. Their scenting capabilities may serve them well in AKC tracking trials. Their responsiveness to trainers' commands and their stamina make them good candidates for agility trials.

Chessies are fine companion dogs, yard dogs, and children's playmates. A well-mannered Chessie is often quite at home on the foot of her child's bed

Fetching a dummy in the backyard is the right beginning of retriever training.

at night. A Canine Good Citizen Award is another type of work that is certainly within the capability of an easily handled Chessie, and some of these versatile retrievers are trained as professional guide dogs for the blind.

AKC hunting tests have been established to rate dogs in their ability to mark and retrieve under actual hunting conditions. The winners are awarded the titles of Junior Hunter, Senior Hunter, and Master Hunter. A tremendous number of Chessies serve the waterfowler's hunting needs, and many are purchased with no intention of competing in hunting tests, but rather for weekend shooting expeditions. They assist their owners in putting ducks and geese on the table for Sunday dinner.

Hunting and Retrieving

This breed has been kept as a gundog for more than a century, and hunting disciplines are natural to most Chessies. Many trainers introduce puppies to feathered dummies when quite young, perhaps five or six weeks of age. Training is then discontinued until a time when the dog's mental maturity indicates that her attention span can handle more intense training. Early conditioning to a hunting life also means training by habituation; accustoming Rosie to gunfire and the smell of gunpowder at an early age.

Two key attributes of a gundog trainer are knowledge and patience. As in other training disciplines, gundog training requires many short, regular practice sessions. There is no right or wrong way to train a dog in any work, and the training technique that is used will depend on the instructor's experience and knowledge. For the average weekend hunter, training your own dog can be fun and rewarding.

"A good retriever is not the work of chance any more than is a good lawyer, doctor or dog trainer" (B. Waters 1895).

Formal gundog retriever training is beyond the scope of this manual but some hints are offered to help you start the pup. If Rosie has inherited the natural retrieving tendencies of the breed, the process is quite simple. It may be started when she is very young, but if she doesn't catch on quickly, wait a week before you try it again. Don't train for more than 15 minutes at a time, and never repeat any exercise so frequently that she loses interest.

Get help if you aren't sure what you are doing; obtain the advice of an experienced gundog trainer; buy a book and follow directions; join a club; but don't, under any circumstances, risk spoiling a fine Chesapeake due to your own lack of knowledge or ability.

To minimize confusion and establish consistency, training should be undertaken by one person if possible. This is doubly important in the case of a situation wherein one member of the family typically plays with the dog and another is responsible for discipline or training. All of the simple obedience commands must be mastered before the dog can begin gun training. Serious training should be delayed until Rosie has reached at least six months of age. Many of the fundamentals may be started earlier, depending upon the mental maturity of your dog.

Dummies

When you begin, use a canvas bumper, a feathered dummy, a soft

Get into the water and invite your pup to join you. A Chessie is rarely reluctant.

ball, or a fabric-covered lightweight object, such as a tennis ball tied in a sock. These are soft to the dog's mouth and will serve you best when teaching your Chessie to retrieve.

Don't "get ahead" of your dog. Never try to teach her more than she is able to grasp. This is especially true in terms of duration of the training sessions. Most trainers say that 5 to 15 minutes each day is ample for any training, and more concentration than that is apt to spoil an otherwise good dog. If you rush your dog, she will become bored and lose her natural sharpness to retrieve.

Note: *Sticks, bones, hard rubber balls, golf balls, or other hard objects should never be used when working or playing with a retriever.* They will encourage Rosie to bite down hard and will promote the development of a "hard mouth" in your Chessie. Her enthusiasm for retrieving will be increased by adding a couple of drops of bird scent on the dummy being used. Scents are available in sporting goods stores, or in a pinch, you can rub a hotdog on the dummy.

Chessies live to hunt.

In the beginning, give Rosie a tidbit as a reward after each successful retrieve. This reinforces the instinctive retriever action of the dog, and elicits better cooperation. After a few sessions, a pat on the head, and a "*Good dog*" takes the place of the reward.

Start your retriever training in the backyard. Attach a 30-foot (9-m) lightweight nylon check cord to her collar and get Rosie's attention by waving the dummy closely in front of her nose. Then toss the dummy a short distance in front of her, accompanying the toss with the "*Rosie, mark*" command, and immediately command "*Fetch*." When she has responded and picked up the dummy, give the command "*Come*" as you gently coax her to return to you by gentle tugs on the check line. When she reaches you, tell her "*Give*," or "*Out*," and take the dummy from her mouth. Don't allow her to drop it. If she refuses to part

with the dummy on command, offer her a tidbit; she can't accept the food without handing you the dummy. Don't forcibly pull the dummy from her; this is no time to play tug-of-war! Then praise her for a job well done, and repeat the exercise.

A variation of this lesson is to work the pup without the long cord. Toss the dummy, and give her the fetch command. Then as she picks the dummy up, begin to run away from her, clapping your hands and telling Rosie "*Come*." As she catches up to you, reach down and take the dummy from her mouth with the command "*Give*."

It is important that you repeat this fetching exercise daily, but not for extended periods of time. Don't allow the dog to become bored with the game. Fetching can sometimes be integrated into her other training sessions when she is taught to *come, sit, stay, whoa*, and other obedience commands.

Scent

Another variation of dummy training will tend to stimulate a Chessie's interest in birds. Obtain a scented bird wing, let her smell it, then toss it into heavy cover or very shallow water. Tell Rosie to mark, then fetch. She should use her eyes as well as her nose to find the wing.

A scented bird wing keeps best in a plastic bag in your freezer when not in use.

Guns

To accustom Rosie to the sound and smell of guns, try a cap pistol or 22-caliber "starting" pistol that shoots only blanks. Fire the gun at a distance from the pup, holding the gun behind you and pointing it away from her. At the sound, she might be slightly startled, but you should ignore her reaction. When she sees that you aren't

Retrieving is done with heads-up swimming.

alarmed, she will be comfortable with the noise. Later, a shotgun can be used. Never fire a gun close to her head; not only will the concussion frighten her, the noise may cause hearing impairment.

Rosie should readily become accustomed to the sound of a gun being fired in her immediate proximity. She should soon master backyard fetching, and her instinctive marking of birds in heavy cover will become as natural as her name. At this time, she is probably ready for her first expedition into the water.

Water Training

Although it is nearly impossible to initiate a fear of water in a Chessie, never toss Rosie into the water. Put on a pair of waders or your bathing suit and walk out into the shallow water of a lake. Call her to come and while squatting down, clap your hands and encourage her to come to you. Play with her and splash about. She will soon be as at home in the water as on land. Water is the Chesapeake's favorite medium, and training her to fetch a floating dummy shouldn't be a problem.

Take your starting pistol and a couple of small bumpers or other floating dummies, and walk with Rosie along a quiet lakeshore or by a pond. Get her attention, tell her "*Rosie, mark,*" toss the dummy in the air, fire the pistol, and give the command "*Fetch.*" When she successfully picks the dummy up from the ground, tell her to come, take the dummy from her, reward her with an ear scratch, and move on. Repeat this procedure using the water as a landing spot for the dummy. You will probably find it second nature for your Chessie to retrieve on land or from the water. Always let her know when she has performed the exercise well, and don't forget that too many lessons will bore Rosie when she is just getting started.

Other exercises that you might try, depending on your style of hunting, are too numerous to discuss in this book. If you hunt from a blind, you must teach Rosie to leave the decoys alone, to jump through a hole in the blind into the water, and to return by the same route. Another exercise that may be necessary is to get into and out of a boat without tipping or capsizing it. There are exercises that are used with netted live pigeons and others that are specific for resolving a hard mouth problem. Others teach the dog to respond to whistle and hand signals.

This discussion of gundog training hardly scratches the surface. Many books have been written on the subject. If you hunt Rosie regularly, you probably will want her professionally trained, or you will join a hunting club and take advantage of their instruction. If you are a seasonal, weekend hunter, you can probably train Rosie yourself, but don't hesitate to confer with friends in the local Chesapeake club.

Retriever Field Trials

A Retriever Field Trial is in the bailiwick of sportsmen, not weekend meat hunters. It is a rapidly growing sport that has spread over the entire country. The American Chesapeake Club held its first field trials in 1932, and together with the Labrador Retriever Club, was the sole promoter of the sport until 1934. In 1935, a retriever trial was held in Illinois, and since then, a steady growth in interest has been seen.

Only AKC-registered, purebred retrievers can run in retriever trials. These trials are intended to prove the value of dogs in the performance of the duties for which they were bred. Like herding trials, tracking trials, and other similar competitions, they test dogs of similar heritage against one another in field performance. They are judged on natural ability, nose, pace, style, determination, drive, and marking ability.

Probably the most important quality of any retriever is her exceptional nose. Her capacity to visually "mark" downed game is of almost equal importance, but exceptional scenting ability is essential. She must be ready to work out the fall of the bird with speed and reach it as quickly as possible. She must be determined to find her bird using her initiative while responding to the commands of her handler. Once the bird is located, it must be tenderly picked up and returned to the handler without hesitation.

Chesapeakes are notoriously water-wise. They rarely hesitate to enter water, regardless of the temperature or roughness. They ordinarily swim high in the water and exhibit great speed when doing so.

A retriever trial offers the fancier another means, another arena in which to exhibit a dog. It is an opportunity to compete the dog against others under field conditions. Retriever owners long ago recognized the importance of competition under a set of rules that was equal for all retrievers and handlers. It gives bragging rights to the owner and handler. It allows one owner to say that his dog is a better retriever than mine, when competing under the same rules with the same judges. With standardized scoring, there is still some degree of interpretation that must be made by the judges, but by applying set rules to certain activities, the best dog usually will come out on top.

Field Champion

The Field Champion title is awarded to a dog that has won a specific number of points in judged trials. The number of entries and the placement of the competing dogs determine the points awarded in the various types of stakes and trials. Briefly, she must win either a National Championship Stake or a total of 10 points earned in other stakes. The formula for awarding the points in the various stakes is complex; to get a full explanation, you may write to the AKC for the Field Trial Rules and Standard Procedure of Retrievers.

The number of dual champion Chesapeakes is small, which doesn't mean that the breed is less well suited for either type of competition. It is simply an indication of the preferences of Chesapeake owners.

Field Trial Classes

There are many different stakes and classes for retrievers that are separated by the dogs' ages and prior wins. According to the AKC Field Trial Rules, the purpose of a trial is to determine the relative merits of retrievers in the field. Retriever field trials should, therefore, simulate as nearly as possible the conditions met in an ordinary day's shoot. The dogs are expected to retrieve any type of game bird under all conditions.

In addition to the retriever trials, once a year the National Retriever Club runs a National Championship Stake. The winner of any such stake is awarded a Field Champion of Record. The National Amateur Retriever Club runs a National Amateur Championship Stake for qualified retrievers each year as well. The winner of that stake is awarded an Amateur Field Champion of Record. In order to win that prestigious award, the handler must be an amateur, as judged by the field trial committee.

Hunting Tests

Retriever clubs may offer Junior, Senior, and Master Hunting Tests for AKC-registered retrievers. These are designed to test the merits of and evaluate the abilities of retrievers in the field to determine their suitability and ability as hunting companions. The dogs are judged in situations as natural as possible, using live game birds, decoys, blinds, and other equipment that would be engaged in actual hunting conditions.

Tests judge the retriever's performance on land and in the water. They are scored on their natural abilities, marking, style, perseverance or courage, and training. The dog's eagerness, manners, response to whistles, handling of birds, and willingness to yield its retrieve are judged. Dogs are not placed (first, second, third, and so on) according to their abilities, but are qualified or not, depending on their own performance.

Obedience Trials

Obedience Trials are competitions for all AKC-registered dogs. In an

Obedience trials can be fun and educational for dog and family.

Obedience trials are excellent training for Chessies.

dogs must be properly trained, but to score well, they must also show "style" and "class" in the many tasks they are given. They must be practiced and smooth, but the judges also look for happy dogs, not robots.

Rules

Obedience trials use many rules to govern the conduct and appearance of competitors. For instance, dogs that have had plastic surgery to correct a congenital defect may participate in obedience trials providing that those dogs have also been neutered. Spaying, castration, or coat defects don't prevent dogs from participating in obedience trials. However, lame or bandaged dogs may not compete, and dogs that have been dyed or artificially colored are ineligible.

If a handler can't control her dog or if she abuses her dog, she will be excused from competition. Handlers who are handicapped may compete in obedience trials under modified rules. Their dogs are required to perform all the usual exercises, but the rules are bent to allow handicapped persons to exhibit their dogs.

Classes, Exercises, and Awards

Novice A Classes and Novice B Classes are for dogs of six months or older that haven't won a Companion Dog (CD) title. Novice exercises consist of heel on leash and figure eight, stand for examination, heel free, recall, long sit, and long down.

The AKC awards a CD title certificate to a dog that has received qualifying scores at three licensed or member obedience trials, under three different judges, providing that at least six dogs were competing in each trial.

Open A Class is for dogs that have won the CD title but haven't won a Companion Dog Excellent title (CDX). The dog's owner or a member of her family must handle the dog.

obedience trial, Rosie may be entered into competition with dozens of dogs of many different breeds.

Obedience trials are designed to demonstrate the usefulness of purebred dogs as companions of the human. They measure the dog's ability to follow a routine and perform certain tasks. Each participant of the various classes performs the same exercises in the same way, and is scored by the judges. The primary objective of obedience trials is to demonstrate the training and conditioning of dogs in every conceivable circumstance. It promotes and displays exemplary dog behavior in all situations in public places in the presence of strange dogs and their handlers.

This sport judges the dogs' willingness and enjoyment of the work as well as the ability to perform according to standards. Obedience trials are very similar to field trials in that the

Open B Class is for dogs that have won the CD title or a CDX title or a UD title (Utility Dog). The owner or any other person may handle these dogs.

The exercises for open classes consist of heel free and figure eight, drop on recall, retrieve on flat, retrieve over high jump, broad jump, long sit, and long down.

A CDX title may be awarded by the AKC to a dog that has received qualifying scores at three obedience trials judged by three different judges.

Utility A Class is for dogs that have won the CDX title but not the UD title. The dogs' owner or member of the immediate family must handle them.

Utility B Class is for dogs that have won the CDX or UD title and any person may handle them.

Utility exercises involve a signal exercise, scent discrimination article 1, scent discrimination article 2, directed retrieve, moving stand and examination, and directed jumping.

A Utility Dog (UD) title is awarded to a dog that has received qualifying scores by three different judges in three obedience trials. There were 55 Chessie Utility Dogs reported in 1985.

Utility dogs may earn points toward the coveted Obedience Trial Championship (OTCh). These points are awarded for each first or second place ribbon won in UD classes, according to the number of dogs competing. A dog must accumulate no less than 100 points under specific circumstances.

A Triple Champion is a dog that has earned a Field Champion title, a Champion of Record title, and an Obedience Trial Championship title.

Tracking Dog

Chessies are also eligible to compete in tracking tests. This is another sport in which Rosie's excellent nose should stand her in good stead.

A track is laid out using articles that are about the size of a glove or wallet.

Agility obstacles are taken in stride.

A stranger to the competing dog lays the track out following a line that has been plotted by a judge. The articles are randomly dropped on the track by the "track layer," so that they can't be seen for more than 20 feet (6 m); neither can they be covered with anything to hide them.

Tracking dogs are kept on long leashes and the handler follows the dog at a distance of no less than 20 feet (6 m). Verbal commands may be given by handlers to encourage the dog, but the handler can't indicate the

Agility trials are another constructive way to have fun with your dog.

different surfaces, including vegetation and two areas devoid of vegetation such as concrete, asphalt, gravel, sand, hard pan, or mulch. No obstacles are used in this test, but tracks may be laid out through distractions such as buildings, breezeways, shelters, and open garages.

There are four articles used in the VST test, each of which is different from the others, and all of which may be easily picked up by the dog. They are made of leather, plastic, metal, and fabric.

Tracking is a sport, and dogs that excel do so because they have highly sensitive noses and enjoy using them. Tracking isn't competitive in the same sense that obedience showing is. There is a camaraderie among handlers, win or lose, and it is a pleasurable event to attend as a spectator. For further information about tracking tests, contact the AKC for their brochure on the subject.

location or direction of the track. There is no time limit on the track but if Rosie stops working the trail, she is marked failed.

Levels and Awards

Tracking Test/TD is for dogs more than six months old that haven't earned a TD, TDX, or VST title. The Tracking Dog (TD) title is earned when a dog is certified by two judges to have passed a Tracking Test/TD.

A Tracking Test/TDX is available to dogs that have already earned a TD title. The Tracking Dog Excellent (TDX) title is awarded to dogs that have been certified by two judges to have passed two Tracking Test/TDX.

The length of track and the complexity of the turns and other items to increase the difficulty of trails are used in the TDX tracks, and even more complexities are included in the Tracking Test/VST.

Variable Surface Tracking (VST) verifies the dog's ability to recognize and follow human scent while adapting to changing scenting conditions. Each track has a minimum of three

Agility Trials

Agility trials are fun contests that demonstrate training, willingness, and energy of dogs as they work with their handlers. Several levels of competition that lead to various titles are included in these trials. They are open to any AKC-registered dog and, as in other AKC events (except conformation shows or field trials), no restrictions are placed on neutered dogs' participation.

In order to enter, the dog must be at least 12 months old, and there are divisions and classes to cover handlers and dogs at every stage of training. The titles earned are Novice Agility (NA), Open Agility (OA), Agility Excellent (AX), and Master Agility Excellent (MX).

Titles and Awards

In order for a dog to earn the titles NA, OA, and AX, she must acquire qualifying scores in three separate trials under two different judges. One title must be earned before the next level of competition is attempted. The MX title is earned after a dog has been awarded the AX title and receives qualifying scores in ten separate trials.

Obstacles

Agility trials use many props and obstacles that are sized according to the size of the dog. There are both broad and high jumps, an A-frame to climb over, an elevated dog walk to traverse, a teetering seesaw to master, a table to pause on, and an open tunnel to go through. There is a closed tunnel made of fabric that the dog must push its way through, a set of poles to weave, and double bar jumps to master. There is also a window that the dog must jump through and an identified area of the ground where the competitor must pause.

Agility obstacles are laid out in a course, and the handler runs along beside, behind, or in front of the dog that is performing. Handlers may not touch the dog at any time. The scoring is based on the course distance, and is timed. A time penalty is awarded for minor infractions and a refusal to try an obstacle counts five points against the participating dog. Refusals are not permitted for dogs that are competing in the AX class.

An agility trial is a spectator sport for all dog enthusiasts, and they have been a source of enjoyment in Europe for many years. They have been catching on very well in the United States in recent times. They are fun for participants and spectators alike, and if you have an active agility club in your area, attend a trial. The participants seem to be having great fun, yet the training that both dogs and handlers undergo is extensive. If you have a Chessie that is biddable and loves to please, agility work may be for you.

Canine Good Citizen Certificate

Dog clubs throughout the United States administer Canine Good Citizen tests for dogs. This program, promoting good manners and behavior, is sponsored by the AKC. Owners can have their dogs evaluated for ten different activities that help to assure that their dogs are good neighbors. There are no points involved; the scoring is a simple pass-or-fail evaluation. The dogs are judged on essential, easily taught activities that include allowing a stranger to approach, walking naturally on a loose lead, walking through a crowd, sitting for examination, reacting to a strange dog, and reacting to a distraction such as a door suddenly closing or a jogger running by the dog.

AKC member clubs make good citizen evaluations, and information about them may be obtained by contacting the AKC or an all-breed club in your community. Having a Canine Good Citizen Certificate hanging on the wall is evidence that your Chessie has been trained. It means that you love your dog enough to spend the time training it, and that Rosie is a good neighbor.

Easy as pie.

Weight pulling is another competitive task for the willing Chessie.

Health Care

Choosing a Good Veterinarian

Every dog owner should be interested in establishing a working relationship with an understanding veterinarian. This professional will have advice about the initial selection of your dog, information regarding routine and specialized care, and an active, aggressive treatment plan for an injured or ill patient that needs veterinary care. The veterinarian is a resource that you can ill afford to be without. The question is how do you choose a good veterinarian?

Ask your dog-owning friends for a reference, then call for an appointment with a local veterinarian before you buy a dog. If you are new in a community or don't know anyone who uses a veterinarian, browse the yellow pages. Don't let the size of the advertisement fool you; many excellent veterinary practitioners don't promote their practice through such ads. When you call, a reliable professional will give you a few minutes of her or his time and will welcome your visit and your inquiries.

When you see the professional, don't waste the veterinarian's time or yours; have a list of questions and ask them. Find out how out-of-hours emergencies are handled. If off-hours treatment is not provided by the veterinarian, and such calls are referred to an emergency care clinic, check it out as well. Ask to take a tour of the animal hospital at a convenient time. Check out the available facilities and equipment and the cleanliness and organization of the hospital.

Choose a doctor and staff who are friendly, caring, and knowledgeable, and are ready to share their knowledge with you. Explain your animal health care needs, and see how the veterinarian responds to them.

Communication is the key to a good relationship with your veterinarian. Locate a clinician who is willing to listen to you. Find one who will spend time explaining procedures and one who isn't too busy to tell you why a recommendation is made. In this prepurchase interview, check on the cost of spaying your female, or castrating your male Chessie. Obtain a fee schedule or inquire about the fees that are charged for routine examinations, vaccinations, fecal exams, and worm treatment. Ask about heartworm, flea, and tick preventive plans and their cost.

It is important to let this professional know that you are placing your trust in him or her, and that you don't take this relationship lightly. The professional should realize that he or she is sharing the stewardship of a pet with you; you are on the same team.

If the veterinarian resists being interviewed or doesn't seem to share your concern about reliable, effective preventive care, you are in the wrong hospital. A veterinarian who has no time for you as a prospective dog owner and client will probably have little time for you after you have acquired a pet.

Once you have purchased your Chessie, check out the doctor's tableside manners. How does the veterinarian handle pets? Does he or she take time for a bit of small talk and a quick rub of a puppy's chin? Does the doctor seem comfortable with your pet?

Using a Veterinarian

Call the veterinarian who performed Rowdy's prepurchase examination and talk with him or her. Better yet, take Rowdy to your own veterinarian for another evaluation. Take the health documents that came from the breeder and ask questions about future vaccination requirements. Ask about Lyme disease, valley fever, or other exotic diseases that may be endemic in your area.

If you haven't yet located a reliable boarding kennel, ask for kennel referrals. If you aren't sure you can clip Rowdy's nails, ask the professional to teach you.

Emergencies

Circumstances that are life threatening are rarely seen in dogs that are confined to a backyard. When the security of a fenced yard is left behind in favor of the hunting field, more emergency situations may be found.

Many of our cars and hunting vehicles are equipped with cellular telephones today. They provide an immediate method of contacting your veterinarian. Be sure to have the correct telephone numbers written on your first-aid kit. When an emergency occurs, evaluate the dog's condition, take the measures suggested, and call your veterinarian for his advice. Let the answering receptionist know that you have an emergency and you're on your way to the hospital, with the approximate time you expect to arrive.

Always carry a first-aid kit when you are out for an afternoon with your dog, whether hunting or hiking. The kit should include boots for the dog, bandages, hydrogen peroxide, a tourniquet, eyewash, tape, and a couple of rolls of gauze. A 4-foot (1.2-m) piece of soft cotton cord such as a venetian-blind cord makes a great muzzle, and should be included in your first-aid kit.

The kit will be small, and ideally should be fastened to your belt. An excellent addition to any first-aid kit is a cellular phone.

Preparing Yourself for an Emergency

Check with your veterinarian about canine first-aid classes that may be given in your area. Attend a series of these classes and practice the emergency procedures on Rowdy at home. An injured dog needs reassurance, the same as an injured person. Keep your voice moderate; speak in low, soothing tones. Never display panic or scream and shout to your companions. Touch the dog's head, pet him, and make him aware that you are trying to help him.

Speed is important when evaluating an emergency; you must be ready to take some calculated action immediately. This means some preparation is necessary on your part. You should be familiar with your dog's normal respiration, pulse, membrane color, body temperature, and other vital signs. You must know the normal vital signs in order to recognize the abnormal.

As a dog owner, you should know how to give Rowdy CPR and how to muzzle him, apply pressure bandages or tourniquets, and carry him.

Restraint is an important part of dealing with an injured dog that is in pain. You must always use the least amount of restraint possible to keep the dog quiet while you examine him. Too much restraint may frighten the dog and make him uncooperative, but in some cases, restraint will be the difference between life and death.

Evaluate First

If Rowdy acts strange, appears "off," and isn't quite himself, whether his illness is discovered at home or in the field, there are certain things you should observe before you call a veterinarian. Take his rectal temperature using either a digital or glass thermometer. The normal range is from 101.5 to 102.5°F (38.5–39.5°C).

Check to see if his breathing is shallow or labored. A dog's normal respiration is between 10 and 30 breaths per minute, and can only be evaluated when he is breathing through his nose, not while he is panting. Is he coughing or sneezing? Does he exhibit a "reverse sneeze," which is not an indication of respiratory distress, but is usually associated with allergy.

Take his pulse. A normal Chesapeake's heart rate is between 70 and 90 beats per minute. The pulse can be taken by pressing your finger against the inside of his thigh, about halfway between his stifle and hip. An alternative way to check heart rate is to firmly press the chest wall at the level of his elbow with your hand.

Look at the color of the membranes of his mouth. Are they a normal shade of pink, or are they dark or pale? Press your finger tightly against his gums. The tissue will turn white with the pressure. Then remove your finger and check the time that the white area takes to reach the normal pink color of the rest of the gums. This is termed the capillary filling time, and should be about two seconds.

Are his eyes normally bright or are they red and inflamed, dull, or discharging pus?

Does he have a normal appetite, and when did he eat last? Have you seen his stool lately, and if so, was it normal? Has he vomited in the recent past, and if so, what did the vomitus look like; was it bloody, mucoid, or filled with foreign material?

Record your observations and call your veterinarian for advice or an appointment. Remember that communication with your health care professional is a two-way street. Don't wait a day or two to see if the dog gets better unless you are advised to do so.

Other Emergencies or Illnesses

Poisoning

If Rowdy has been poisoned, waste no time in getting him to a veterinarian. If you are able to locate some of the poisonous agent, or a label from the container, take it with you. If the label instructs you to induce vomiting, you can do so by placing about a teaspoonful of salt on the back of the dog's tongue. A tablespoonful of hydrogen peroxide may be administered orally, which will also produce vomiting. Syrup of epicac may be used, but it frequently is slow to work.

Car Accidents

A dog that has been hit by an automobile constitutes an emergency, regardless of where it occurs. These dogs usually require professional help. First, control any visible hemorrhage, then wrap the dog up. Keep him quiet and warm. If he is exhibiting pain, muzzle him before handling. Shock, with or without internal hemorrhage, is always a serious consideration when an automobile has struck a dog. Use a board, jacket, or blanket as a stretcher to transport Rowdy to the veterinarian. Time is of the essence!

Seizures

Epilepsy is the most common cause of convulsive seizures. They often begin after a year or two of age, and may come at any time. If the dog has no history of epilepsy, try to ascertain the cause of his seizure. It may be the result of a head injury or poisoning. In any case, try to prevent Rowdy from injuring himself; wrap him in a blanket or coat and waste no time getting him to the veterinary hospital.

HOW-TO:
Treat Emergencies

Every dog owner should learn fundamental canine CPR methods.

Shock

Dogs in shock don't always look the same; they may be prostrate or relatively alert, tense and anxious or weak and staggering, overheated or cold.

The usual signs of shock include pale gums and tongue, rapid, shallow respiration, slow capillary filling time, and a rapid heart rate of usually more than 150 beats per minute.

Causes of shock are also quite variable; hemorrhage or internal bleeding, severe trauma with or without broken bones, twisted stomach (see Gastric Torsion, page 80), severe animal bites, poisons, deep puncture wounds, and snake bite are all causes of shock.

When shock is suspected, control bleeding, keep the patient warm, and get him to a veterinarian quickly.

Cardiopulmonary resuscitation (CPR) may be used if a dog's heart has stopped. Lay the dog on his right side, and with the heel of your hand press downward to compress his chest immediately behind his elbow for half a second, then release.

For artificial respiration, clean the dog's mouth of mucus and debris. Tilt his head back, hold his mouth shut with your hand, and place your mouth over his muzzle. Blow into the dog's nose until you see his chest begin to expand. Release your hand and allow him to exhale and repeat every five seconds.

If Rowdy is bleeding profusely, find the source and apply a pressure bandage. Keep him quiet. Obtain a blanket or use your jacket as a stretcher for the injured dog. In order to prevent further damage, it is important to handle the dog minimally.

Muzzle

Before attempting to evaluate or treat serious or extensive injuries, consider muzzling a hurt dog. Any pet may snap or bite viciously when he is frightened, hurt, or in shock, or feels threatened. Approach him slowly, lower yourself to his level, and speak to him in a soft voice. Avoid direct eye contact with him and if he shows the

Place the pressure bandage over the wound, and secure it snugly to control hemorrhage.

slightest apprehension or aggression, apply a muzzle before you go any further.

Tie a single loose knot in the center of the length of cord and slip this loop over the dog's muzzle. Pull the knot snugly on top of his muzzle, just below the stop. Take the ends of the cord beneath his muzzle and tie another single knot. Then take the ends of the cord behind his ears and tie it snugly in place. If you don't have a muzzle cord in your first-aid kit, tear a piece of gauze about 4 feet (1.2 m) long from a bandage roll and substitute it for the cord.

Cuts and Lacerations

A hard-running retriever will sometimes encounter barbed wire shards that have been torn from a fence and lie hidden in the weeds or under the surface of the water. The lacerations that result may be nothing more than minor scratches or small skin tears that can wait a few hours for treatment, or they may cause more serious wounds. Examine the dog carefully to determine how extensive the wound is. If the skin tear is significant (more than an inch long), put a leash on the dog and call a halt to the hunting.

If the laceration is large and particularly if it extends deeply into the muscle, either hold Rowdy still and bring your car to him, or pick him up and carry him to the car. Don't allow him to run back to the car. Further contamination of the wound from tiny weed seeds and other debris will be difficult to wash away.

Place a pressure bandage over a bleeding wound to control the hemorrhage, or control the bleeding with finger pressure if a bandage can't be placed on the wound. A tourniquet is the last resort and should be used only when there is no other way to stop the bleeding. If a tourniquet is used, tighten it only enough to stop the hemorrhage and release it for a few seconds every 15 to 20 minutes.

Gunshot

If a dog is accidentally shot with a shotgun, the damage that results is relative; it will depend on the distance from which he was shot, the type of load, the gauge of the shotgun, and the part of his body the pellets struck. If he was many yards away and took a few pellets in his rump, the damage isn't likely to be great. If he was close to the gun and some of the pellets struck him in the face, chest, or abdomen, you must assume that an emergency exists. There is very little you can do in the field except keep him warm and quiet; waste no time in getting the dog to a veterinarian.

Snake Bite

If Rowdy suffers a rattlesnake or other poisonous viper bite,

Use your coat as a stretcher to carry a badly injured dog to the car.

immediately stop the dog, restrain him with a short leash, and pick him up. Keep him totally quiet, carry him to the car, and get him to your veterinarian as quickly as possible. Snake venom enters the bloodstream and travels quickly in an active animal. There will be some swelling and tissue damage at the site of the bite, but don't cut and mutilate the area. Likewise, a tourniquet is usually contraindicated. Ice packs are sometimes used over the bite wound to slow the venom's travel but it is a mistake to freeze the tissue.

Your veterinarian may dispense antivenin to carry in your first-aid kit if poisonous snakes

Hunting boots should be custom fitted and laced snuggly onto all four of the Chessie's feet.

are common in your hunting area. The directions for its use will accompany the antivenin vials. This product is quite expensive, has a short storage life, and requires several doses for larger dogs.

Punctures

A deep puncture wound is another cause for alarm. When the wound involves the chest area, abdomen, or upper leg, it may present an emergency. If a sharp stick has broken off and remains in the dog, leave it alone. Pick the dog up and carry him to your car and transport him to the veterinarian. If you attempt to remove the stick, you might cause increased hemorrhage or you may leave a tiny piece of the stick lodged deep in the tissues where it is difficult to locate.

If the cause of the puncture isn't visible, apply a pressure bandage to control bleeding and get to the veterinarian immediately.

Footpad Lacerations

Lacerated pads are injuries that may be serious or minor, depending on their extent. Most hunting dogs cut a pad at some time in their careers, and rarely are such wounds life threatening. If the pad laceration is extensive and continues into the web, stop the hemorrhage with a light pressure bandage and put Rowdy in his crate until he can be seen by the veterinarian. If the laceration is small, confined to a single pad, and hemorrhage control isn't a factor, it is OK to put his protective boots on and continue to hunt if Rowdy is willing.

Preventive Medicine

The breeder usually begins a series of vaccinations soon after puppies are weaned. These vaccinations should be continued throughout the dog's life. The particular vaccination schedule for Rowdy should be designed for him and his lifestyle.

The following discussion relates to infectious diseases that are contagious and may be prevented by vaccinations that are given at the appropriate time.

Canine Distemper (CD)

Canine distemper (CD), dog plague or hard pad, continues to be a significant threat to young puppies. Its mortality rate, lack of cure, and easy transmission make it an important canine disease. A virus that attacks the dog's respiratory tract, intestinal tract, and brain causes CD. This disease often results in nervous problems, convulsions, and death. The reservoir for infection of CD often exists in stray dog populations and wild carnivores such as raccoons, foxes, and minks.

CD may cause sudden death in puppies, with few if any visible symptoms. In older dogs, signs of infection include fever, loss of appetite, lethargy, dehydration, diarrhea, and vomiting. A yellow or green ocular discharge often accompanies CD, and coughing is another common sign of the disease. Some dogs may seem to respond to various treatments, only to succumb to convulsions and paralysis at a later date. Hardened footpads, tooth enamel deficiencies, and permanent neurological signs such as blindness or twitching of extremities often affect those dogs that miraculously survive the disease.

Don't neglect your puppy's vaccinations! The first of a series of CD vaccinations is given at about six weeks of age, and the vaccine is usually combined with other vaccines. To maintain a protective level of immunity, annual boosters are required. Keep Rowdy confined and away from any possible exposure until he has had at least his first two vaccinations.

Hepatitis

Infectious canine hepatitis is another contagious, incurable, fatal disease of dogs. It is highly communicable among dogs, but is not contagious to humans. Now known by the initials CAV-1 (canine adenovirus, type 1), it is a systemic disease that causes severe liver damage. Symptoms often mimic those of distemper and it may cause sudden death in young pups.

Vaccines are highly effective in preventing canine hepatitis and are usually combined with other immunizing agents. A series of vaccinations is begun at or shortly after six weeks of age, with annual boosters required

Leptospirosis

Lepto is a kidney disease that is sometimes fatal, and is caused by a spirochete organism that is similar to a bacterium. This highly contagious infection is transmitted by urine from affected animals and it can infect humans as well as other animals. It is more prevalent in male dogs than in females.

Signs of a lepto infection include lethargy, lack of appetite, thirst, rusty-colored urine, diarrhea, and vomiting. Affected dogs sometimes walk with a peculiar stilted, roach-backed gait. Treatment of lepto may be effective, but permanent kidney damage resulting from an infection can be serious. Leptospirosis vaccine is usually combined with CD and CAV-1 immunizing products.

Parvo and Corona Viruses

Canine parvovirus and coronavirus are two of the more recently discovered contagious, and often fatal, canine diseases. Both cause severe diarrhea, vomiting, dehydration, and depression, and they are especially dangerous to puppies. They are spread from infected dogs by saliva, feces, vomit, or one-on-one contact. Humans are not susceptible to these viruses, but they may transmit the disease on their shoes or clothes.

Supportive therapy improves the prognosis, but in young animals, sudden death is common. If the vomiting and diarrhea are treated and dehydration is successfully controlled with intravenous fluid therapy, the dog may live.

Vaccinations are usually given at the same time as the other immunizations, at or shortly after six weeks of age, with annual boosters also required. Consult with your veterinary practitioner about the use of those products.

Kennel Cough

Parainfluenza virus and *Bordetella* bacteria cause coughing, fever, loss of appetite, and depression. They are highly contagious and are easily spread by aerosol (airborne droplets of saliva in an affected dog's cough or sneeze). The dog's bronchial tubes, trachea, and throat are affected.

Uncomplicated kennel cough may pass in a couple of weeks if the dog is rested and isolated and the associated bacterial infections are treated. Kennel cough typically has a lower fatality rate than some of the diseases that were previously discussed, but it deserves serious consideration in your vaccination program.

Respiratory vaccines include intranasal types that are often less predictable than injectables, but their reliability is improving. Because of recent advances in vaccine research, consult with your local veterinarian about what product is best in your situation.

Lyme Disease

This relatively new disease of the dog and human population is vec-

tored or carried by the deer tick. In the past, Lyme disease was more common in the northeastern and mid-western areas of the United States, but it has now spread nationwide, and is presently known to exist in 40 states. White-tailed deer and field mice are the principal reservoir hosts for the disease.

Lyme disease often causes lameness in the dog and is accompanied by heat, pain, and swelling of one or more joints. Body temperature is usually elevated, and affected dogs are listless. Early treatment is vital if the dog is to be returned to normal.

The risk of Lyme disease is related to the length of time that a tick is attached to your dog. When you find a tick on Rowdy, take it off immediately. (See Ticks in the discussion of external parasites, page 84.) When you are in an area where deer ticks are seen, check your dog at least daily for their presence. They are tiny, about 0.1 inch (.04 cm) diameter, black, or red and black, and they often look like a little mole on the skin. As they suck blood, they grow much larger, grayer, with the female ticks sometimes reaching the size of a grape.

There is a Lyme disease vaccine available but its efficacy is questionable. Check with your veterinarian. Newer vaccines against Lyme disease are being produced, and may be available by the time this book is in print. A good tick preventive program is essential in any case

Rabies

Rabies is a fatal disease of warm-blooded animals caused by a virus. It is spread primarily by contact with the saliva of an infected animal; therefore, it usually is associated with bite wounds. The signs of rabies reflect brain changes. The average time lapse between an infected bite and signs of the disease (incubation period) is

Chessies are at home in the field.

ties have ordinances or laws that require rabies vaccinations to be administered when dogs reach three months of age by, or under the direction of, licensed and USDA-accredited veterinarians. Those laws are made to address the public health significance of the disease.

Reservoirs of rabies virus are found in wild animals such as skunks, foxes, raccoons, coyotes, bats, and other wildlife. Because this incurable and fatal disease can be transmitted to humans and all other warm-blooded animals, great emphasis is placed on rabies preventive programs.

Other Common Diseases

Gastric Torsion, Dilatation, and Bloat

Gastric torsion is commonly seen in breeds that are Chessie size and larger. There are many theories as to the cause of this often fatal condition. Allowing your dog to exercise after eating a heavy meal is a factor that promotes gastric torsion. Another is the practice of feeding the dog on the floor or ground, followed by activity.

About two to six hours after a meal, an affected dog begins to display abdominal bloat. Its stomach becomes distended and twisted on its long axis, which prevents the gas from escaping. The patient repeatedly attempts to vomit, but is unable to do so and produces only thick saliva in small amounts. A veterinarian may attempt to pass a stomach tube to relieve the stomach gas, but due to the twist, those efforts are often futile.

The dog quickly goes into shock and staggers, and the bloat causes intense abdominal pain. Immediate surgery may save the pet, but unfortunately by the time the dog reaches a veterinary hospital, he may be suffering from advanced toxemia and efforts to save the patient may be too late.

usually only two or three weeks but occasionally it is several months. The rabies virus travels from the site of the bite to the brain by way of nerves. If the infecting bite occurs on a foot, it results in a longer incubation period. After reaching the brain, the rabies virus migrates to the salivary glands where it reproduces.

The signs of rabies in a dog are varied. Sometimes the affected dog becomes aggressive and highly irritable. As the disease progresses, the dog may become paralyzed (dumb rabies) or vicious (furious rabies).

Vaccine for this important disease is usually administered later than other diseases. Many cities and coun-

There are a number of measures you can take that will help prevent this condition from developing. Feed your dog when his activity is at a minimum. Elevate his food bowl to minimize swallowing air. Encourage frequent, small meals (free choice feeding). When you feed the major meal of the day, make sure that your Chessie is quiet thereafter. Don't allow the dog to engorge with water following a meal. Above all, curtail Rowdy's activity after any meal.

Grass Awns

Whether your pet enjoys the freedom of a fenced yard or is a hunting companion, he is bound to encounter the nuisance of cheat grass or wild oats. The seeds of those plants are called awns and are attached to little beards that catch in your socks when you walk though the grass. Those same little bearded awns can make their way into Rowdy's ears, causing great discomfort and necessitating a trip to your veterinarian for removal.

Grass awns also may catch in the hair between Rowdy's toes. If not discovered and removed promptly, the sharply pointed little seeds penetrate the skin and begin to migrate into the tissue, requiring minor surgery to remove them.

Intestinal Parasites

Those parasites that live in a dog's intestinal tract cause nutritional problems and physical irritation that affect the condition and attitude of the host. Parasites such as tapeworms, roundworms, whipworms, hookworms, and coccidia may seriously affect the general health and vitality of puppies.

Roundworm larvae may remain hidden in cysts in female dogs' tissues throughout their lives. During pregnancy, larvae migrate from their cysts into the unborn puppies and develop in the growing pups' intestines, where

Have your Chessie checked for heartworm.

they mature and produce eggs. Roundworm eggs in a dog's feces are the sources of infestation for other dogs (and possibly under certain rare circumstances, for children). These and other parasite ova (eggs) are identified upon microscopic examination of puppies' feces.

A Chesapeake charging to make a retrieve.

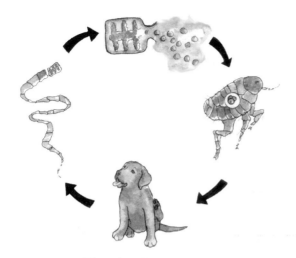

Life cycles of common canine intestinal parasites.

A stool sample from your Chessie should be taken to your veterinarian at least once a year. If parasite ova are found in the stool sample, your veterinarian will prescribe an appropriate medication for treatment.

Tapeworms require secondary hosts. They aren't transmitted from dog to dog as are other parasites. Tapeworms use deer, ground birds, rodents, or fleas as their secondary host. To become infected, the dog must eat part of one of these hosts. Fleas are probably the most common secondary host of tapeworms, and eating an infected flea can transmit the tapeworm to dogs.

This parasite can't usually be diagnosed by a stool sample. The tapeworm head remains attached to the lining of the dog's intestine. Its body is made up of segments and the worm grows to enormous lengths. As it grows, the segments break off and pass out in the stool. Diagnosis is made by finding small white segments of the tapeworm that look like tiny grains of rice, which are often stuck to the hair around the dog's anus.

Treating Worms

Remember that worm medications are types of poisons. For the average Chesapeake owner, it is best to leave the worm treatment to the trained veterinarian. If medication is dispensed by your veterinarian, be meticulous when calculating dosages and carefully administer the medication according to label directions.

An especially perilous procedure is to "worm" all puppies, whether or not a parasite infestation has been diagnosed. If Rowdy isn't harboring parasites, don't treat him. There is no excuse for doing something well that shouldn't be done at all.

Heartworms

Heartworm larvae are transmitted from an infected dog by mosquitoes. These microscopic immature worms develop in the mosquito for a couple of weeks, and are then injected into another dog when the mosquito bites it. The larvae mature into adult heartworms that have reached up to a foot in length and are the diameter of a matchstick, and live in the dog's heart. There may be no immediate outward signs of disease if only a few are present, but in heavy infestations the dog may show dynamic symptoms of heart failure. An infected dog acts as a reservoir of infection for other dogs.

Heartworm disease was originally found in areas where there were lakes, rivers, and bays, the normal habitat for Chesapeakes. In recent years, the disease has spread to nearly every part of the United States including Alaska. Before a preventive program can be initiated, a blood test must show that there are no larvae circulating in your dog's bloodstream. Heartworm prevention is accomplished by means of regular oral medication.

Mosquitoes often bite the short-haired areas of a dog's body, such as his face, legs, and ears. Your Chessie's thick, oily coat is not protection against heartworm.

External Parasites

Skin fungus (ringworm) and mite infestations (mange) are often seen in weanling puppies. There are various fungi that may denude the skin, and several mites that may cause skin lesions that appear the same as the fungal infections. The most common mange mites are *Cheyletiella, Demodex, Psoroptes*, and *Sarcoptes*. Another mite, *Otodectes,* may parasitize ear canals of both cats and dogs.

Allergies, nutritional problems, hormonal imbalances, surface irritations, tumors, and parasites may cause dermatological (skin) disorders. They are commonly mistaken for one another and mistreated. A definitive diagnosis must be made before any treatment program is started. Skin scrapings that are examined under a microscope will identify the mites responsible for mange lesions. Examination of earwax will identify ear mites. Skin scrapings, ultraviolet light, or cultures are used to identify fungal infections.

Pediculosis is the term used to describe a louse infestation. Lice may be of the sucking or biting varieties. They are easily diagnosed and treated, because all life stages of the louse live on the dog, and topical treatment such as dips or medicated baths are usually satisfactory therapy.

Don't rely on a universal mange dip or ringworm salve to cure skin diseases. Those products may create new problems while doing nothing toward solving the initial one.

Fleas

Probably the most irritating parasite is also the most common one. It is seen in backyard or kenneled dogs, and heavy infestations are found in warmer, more humid climates. This parasite lives part of its life cycle off

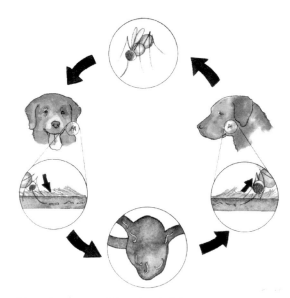

Mosquitoes are an integral part of the heartworm life cycle.

the dog, and is therefore more difficult to treat successfully than lice. Fleas are secondary hosts for tapeworms and the fleas' saliva often causes an allergic dermatitis in dogs that is confusing to diagnose and difficult to treat.

Fleas bite, making a small wound in the skin, then lap up the blood as it oozes from the wound. Adult fleas have the ability to leap great distances, and they sometimes land on a human. They aren't terribly particular where they receive their blood meal, but fleas will usually be found on a dog when one is available. One way to locate fleas is to use a fine-tooth comb and carefully run it through Rowdy's coat over his pelvis. The parasites will be caught between the flea comb's teeth, or will jump from his hair in front of the comb. If the adult fleas aren't found, you may see some of their excreta (feces), which appear as tiny, black, comma-shaped debris.

Bringing home the duck.

There are now several new flea-repellent products available from your veterinarian. Some are in tablet form and are given orally. Others are in liquid form that is applied topically on the skin once a month. Some kill the flea eggs; others only kill the adult. Ask your veterinarian about the products, their safety, cost, and effectiveness.

New biological control programs are presently being initiated in some areas. One involves the yard application of tiny nematodes (worms) that consume flea eggs but are harmless to humans and pets. Others involve the use of insect growth regulators that interfere with the flea's life cycle.

A new generation of flea collars are also available that repel the parasites, rather than killing them after they have bitten the dog and caused their damage.

Organic products such as pyrethrum and other "natural" insecticides are usually thought of as safer. That may or may not be the case, but they are less effective than the contemporary products. A collar is available that emits high frequency sounds that are supposed to repel fleas, but its effectiveness is suspect.

Do not use oral medication, dips, sprays, powders, medicated collars, or other drugs that are not labeled for the specific age and weight of your Chessie. Talk to your veterinarian about the use of all systemic medications in a pregnant or lactating female.

Ticks

Adult ticks bury their heads in a dog's skin and suck blood for days at a time. The males are tiny little fellows, about the size of a pinhead. The females often reach the size of a grape when they fill with blood. After a blood meal, they fall off, lay thousands of eggs, and die. Their other life stages may be completed on the dog (as in the brown dog tick), or they may

Fleas are quite irritating to the dog, whether they cause an allergy or not. They are often responsible for Rowdy's licking, chewing, and scratching, and the formation of "hot spots," another serious skin condition.

If faced with a flea problem, remember that this parasite is a part-time resident of the dog. Once it arrives on its host, it feeds, mates, and lays eggs. The eggs are deposited on the dog, and fall off in the doghouse, on your carpet, or wherever Rowdy happens to be. The eggs hatch into larvae that feed on dandruff and other organic debris in their environment. They pupate, and emerge to begin looking for a host. The adult flea can live for more than 100 days without a blood meal.

If fleas are diagnosed, be sure to follow a long-term treatment program that uses products that are proven safe for the age of your Chessie.

use birds, deer, rodents, or other mammals for secondary hosts.

If you find a tick on Rowdy, grasp it as close to his skin as possible with a pair of tweezers or forceps. With firm, steady traction, pull it out. Ticks are often found under the collar, under the forelegs, around the ears, and over the withers.

Don't panic if the tick's head breaks off. Contrary to popular belief, the imbedded part of the tick that remains in the dog may cause a minor local infection but no systemic problem. After you have extracted the tick, destroy it by placing it in alcohol. Don't try to drown a tick in water, don't squash it, and don't handle the tick with your bare fingers.

Where the tick was imbedded, clean the skin with alcohol once or twice daily for several days. This will keep the scab off and allow drainage from the wound that the tick left.

A common belief is that ticks will be forced to detach if you heat their bodies with the flame of a match or the hot tip of a soldering iron. Heat really doesn't hasten their exit and the heat may be hazardous to your dog. You may hear that if a drop of acetone, alcohol, or nail polish remover is placed on the tick, it will release its hold quickly. The theory is that the rapid evaporation of such products cools the tick and causes it to release its hold. That idea has more credibility than heating the tick, but it doesn't work every time.

Tick-borne Diseases

Lyme disease was discussed under Preventive Medicine (see page 00). Ehrlichiosis is another tick-borne disease to be reckoned with. It is transmitted by the brown dog tick, and is a serious disease, manifested by nosebleeds, swelling of the limbs, anemia, and a multitude of other signs. It can be fatal if not treated early and adequately.

The loathesome tick can transmit several serious dog diseases.

Hereditary Conditions

Monorchidism

Male dogs are born with both testicles positioned in their abdomens. Soon after birth, or by 30 or 40 days of age, the testicles should be descended into a male puppy's scrotum. Monorchidism occurs when one testicle is retained in the dog's abdomen and the other is normally descended. Testicular retention is hereditary, but the genetic mechanism is poorly understood.

Monorchid males are able to breed and are fertile. Such dogs should be castrated at or soon after puberty because retained testicles often develop malignant tumors. Due to the hereditability of monorchidism, males with a retained testicle should never be used in a breeding program.

Cryptorchidism

Cryptorchids are males with both testicles retained in the abdomen. They are typically sterile but not impotent; they will mount and breed females, but usually are unable to produce offspring. Cryptorchid dogs should be castrated at or shortly after reaching puberty to prevent the development of malignant tumors later in life. Cryptorchidism is occasionally reported in Chesapeakes.

85

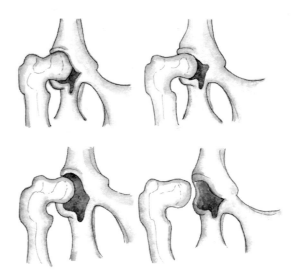

Canine hip dysplasia is a crippling disease that doesn't usually cause symptoms until the dog is an adult.

Epilepsy

Epilepsy is a convulsive disorder that is thought to be inherited. It may also result from injury, tumors, or possibly certain infections, but generally it must be considered genetic in origin. Unfortunately, the condition doesn't show up until the affected dog is several years old, so the inherited condition is difficult to breed out of a strain or bloodline. Epilepsy is rarely reported in Chessies.

Canine Hip Dysplasia (CHD)

A controversial disease, canine hip dysplasia (CHD) causes hind leg lameness that sometimes doesn't appear until the dog is an adult. CHD, or a predisposition to it, is undoubtedly hereditary, but in a complex way. It is prevalent to some degree in all large and in many small purebred dogs. Dogs that have their hips X-rayed, have those X-rays checked by the Orthopedic Foundation for Animals (OFA), and are certified clear of the disease may (but rarely) produce affected puppies. In fact, CHD may crop up in dogs from bloodlines that are certified "clear" for several generations.

CHD involves the head of the femur and the acetabulum (pelvic hip socket). As the disease develops, the acetabulum and femoral head are often malformed and don't fit together as they should. In time, arthritis usually results from the condition, causing pain, inflammation, and lameness.

CHD is a relative condition, and all dogs aren't equally affected. The degree of lameness depends on the amount of displacement of the femoral head and the degree of damage to the cartilage that has been caused by the deformity. Signs of the disease usually appear clinically by two or three years of age, but occasionally they are delayed as late as six or seven years. Signs of CHD may appear in one hind leg (unilateral) or both hind legs (bilateral) causing pain, difficulty in getting up from a lying or sitting position, and lameness when walking. It may progress to a level wherein the dog can't get up or walk. Those dogs are usually thin, and are in pain most of the time.

Treatments include hip replacement, other surgical techniques to relieve pain, acupuncture, anti-inflammatory drugs, and more recently poly-sulfated glycosaminoglycan (PSGAG), with or without chondroitin. This product seems to stimulate the repair of cartilage and shows promise. None of the treatments or medication will cure the disease, and only the prudent selection of breeding stock can prevent the condition from occurring. X-rays that are taken before the dog is two years of age are not conclusive.

The Chessie has a significant incidence of CHD. It is recommended that all breeding stock be OFA certified clear before mating.

The OFA address is listed in Useful Addresses and Literature, page 100.

Progressive Retinal Atrophy (PRA)

Progressive retinal atrophy (PRA) is a serious hereditary eye disease. It is caused by degeneration of retinal cells, and leaves the dog unable to see stationary objects. It usually causes vision impairment signs by about five years of age.

Examination of breeding stock for these diseases is critically important. (Ask your veterinarian about the various certifying agencies such as CERF, listed in Useful Addresses and Literature, page 99.) A few affected dogs can be treated, but cure is unlikely. A dog affected with PRA may lose its vision, but blindness isn't fatal. If the vision diminishes slowly, the dog will adapt and live a normal life span as a pet.

PRA is occasionally reported in the Chessie.

Entropion

Entropion may develop at any age, and although it is not a serious threat to the life or health of the dog, it is hereditary and affected dogs shouldn't be bred.

This condition consists of excess skin around the dog's eyes that causes the lids of the eyes (upper or lower) to roll inward. When this condition occurs, the hair of the eyelids rubs on the dog's cornea, causing severe irritation. Secondary bacterial infection usually accompanies entropion, and the dog often squints in discomfort.

The condition can be repaired with a relatively simple operation. This surgery is usually effective, although if the dog's skin is extremely loose around the eyes, a second operation may be necessary.

Other hereditary diseases that are reported to occur in the Chessie are cerebellar abiotrophy, overbite, and underbite.

Diseases of the Aging Chessie

Brood Bitch Diseases

If your Chessie has had no health problems, and has raised puppies, she should be retired by six or seven years of age. If breeding or whelping complications of any kind occurred, earlier retirement is prudent. Although menopause does not occur in canines, reproductive lives of females end much earlier than those of males. By about six years of age, a Chessie dam has usually passed her productive peak, although she continues to cycle and exhibit normal heat periods. Reproductive problems and the bitch's health risks are likely to increase with each passing year.

The best advice for Chessie owners is to retire your brood bitch before serious maladies of age begin to show up. When the decision is made to retire her from reproductive or showing duties, schedule an ovariohysterectomy (spay). Spay operations in older females are somewhat more

Retire from hunting? Not me, I'm Ethel the wonder dog!

monly in older females. This infectious disease is sometimes fatal in young and middle-age females, but its danger is multiplied many times in older animals. It can be averted by ovariohysterectomy.

Pyometra is an extremely dangerous type of uterine infection and occurs most commonly in aged unspayed females.

Mammary Tumors

Breast tumors account for nearly half of all canine tumor cases, and at least half of these are malignant. They may occur at any age, but are more common in females past six years old. If spayed at or before puberty, the risk of mammary tumors is negligible, but each time the female comes in heat, her predisposition for tumors increases.

Euthanasia

Putting a dog to sleep is a subject we all hate to discuss. It would be convenient if our old dogs wouldn't suffer from their infirmities, and when their time is up, they would lay down and die. Unfortunately, it doesn't often happen that way. That's the reason for euthanasia; it's the final act of kindness, of stewardship, that we can perform for our canine companions. When the lethal product is administered properly, a dog suffers no fear or apprehension. Your veterinarian will give your pet an injection, and its life will be over in a few seconds. You can stay with your old Chessie to the last, or go to another room—that's up to you. If you are going to cry and fall apart at the seams, it's probably easier on the dog if you stay away. If you can hold the animal, giving calm assurance, it's better if you are there. In any case, euthanasia, in competent hands, may be better than watching your pet die slowly from an incurable illness.

difficult to perform, and there are slightly higher risks involved than in young animals, but those risks are minor compared to the risks of pyometra, tumors, and mammary cancer. *Ovariohysterectomy is the best insurance policy you can buy for your retired female Chessie.*

Metritis and Pyometra (Uterine Infection)

Metritis and pyometra are diseases that frequently affect unspayed bitches. Dystocias (difficult births), combined with prolonged labor, seem to increase the probability of uterine infections. Metritis occurs most com-

Breeding Your Chessie

Few people buy their first Chessie with the idea of breeding her and raising puppies. Many established breeders started out with a pet or companion dog, and became fascinated with the breed later. They discovered that Chessie breeding offers a world of memorable experiences; it is a rewarding hobby. Exhibiting their dogs and watching them win ribbons and titles are thrills that are surpassed only by raising a truly fine litter of Chessie puppies. Unfortunately, there are many downsides to that story that must be considered.

Reasons for Breeding

Breeding good purebred dogs correctly is an expensive hobby. As a companion or gundog, the Chesapeake is relatively popular at this time and this acceptance encourages many greedy amateurs to enter the breeding scene, looking for a fast buck. They denigrate the breed, flooding the market with average and below average dogs. Too many times, a cute seven-month-old female is bred to a neighbor's nice little one-year-old male with disastrous results. If both parents are AKC registered, the pups are all eligible for registration, regardless of their quality. They are offered to the public as AKC-registered Chessies and every fault and hereditary deformity imaginable may be propagated. If your motive is primarily monetary, you might be surprised to learn how little

Taking the pups to the field to make a choice. Unfortunately, they both prefer laps.

money is realized from dog breeding when it is done right.

The only legitimate reason for breeding your Chessie is to improve the breed and to produce excellent quality show or field dogs. To be successful, you must strive to raise puppies that have uniformly predictable, trustworthy temperaments. If you can't do that, better give it up. Only the best females should be bred to the very best males. To do less isn't fair to the beautiful Chessie.

You can't raise show-quality pups from a pet-quality dam or sire. If the dam hasn't proved herself in shows, trials, or under the gun, the chances are good that her puppies will do no better. It isn't likely that you will raise pups with great temperaments from a bitch or sire that is difficult to handle. Hopefully, before entering into a breeding program, you will consider those sobering thoughts.

If you decide to produce a litter from your female, draw up a plan. Establish in advance the probable markets for your pups. There are several pet-quality pups in every litter; be certain that you can place all the pups in good homes before you progress any further. Do your homework; discover how many Chessie puppies are presently offered for sale in your area. Should you breed her now, or will it be better to wait six months?

Breeding Stock Selection

Veterinary examinations of the prospective parents will reveal major hereditary faults, but it is recommended that you go a step further before you embark on a career in Chesapeake breeding. Every bitch has a few shortcomings that may influence the selection of a stud. Ask a successful Chessie breeder to fault your dog. If you are primarily interested in conformation shows, this might be someone with experience

in judging or showing the breed. If your bitch is primarily a hunter, ask the advice of trainers and handlers that are experienced with field trials or gundogs. Slight discrepancies from the breed standard are expected, because there is no such thing as a perfect Chessie. If both sire and dam display the same minor imperfections, however, their progeny may exhibit major faults.

Your bitch and the chosen sire should be physically examined, preferably by the same veterinarian, who is furnished with breeding and health histories of both animals. This health care professional will want to examine for, or see certifications of, normal hip conformation for both the male and female. Keep in mind that OFA hip certification isn't done until the dogs are more than two years old. Congenital eye diseases as well as other hereditary problems should be considered.

A maiden bitch should ideally be bred to a proven stud if available; one that has produced excellent pups from previous matings. Hopefully he will have sired pups from a bitch that is related to yours. The quality of his progeny is one measure of his value. His conformation, temperament, and ability should be exemplary.

Pedigree Examination

Genetic considerations must be studied before a bitch is bred. Her background should be compatible with the sire's. If they are distantly related, that should present no problem, but inbreeding and linebreeding should be left to the experts. As a novice breeder, it would be well for you to again enlist the assistance of an experienced breeder. Study the pedigrees of both sire and dam in detail. Look at pictures and the accomplishments of the dogs that are listed thereon. Don't fall into the many traps that ensnare beginners, such as the notion that if a dog wins its championship, it is bound to produce champions.

If you bought your female as the most promising pup of a good litter and she has lived up to your expectations, she may be a good brood bitch. If you breed her to a proven male with a similar background—one that has produced excellent puppies from a bitch with a pedigree that is similar to your bitch's—you might be on a roll.

Finding Good Homes for Pups

Before you breed your bitch, consider the six to eight puppies that will result from the breeding. If you are active in either a breed or hunting club, you're not likely to encounter any problem finding good homes for most of your puppies. Those pups that remain after the best prospects are gone are equally entitled to good homes. If you planned well, the pet-quality pups should be placed into companion dog homes or with weekend shooters. Advertising in newsletters will usually locate additional placements, but you should always interview prospective buyers before you release a pup to a new home.

Be sure the buyers know what they are getting. If the pup isn't outstanding, make the buyers aware that it is not a breeding or showing prospect. Consider withholding registration, limited registration, or co-ownership of the pet-quality pup until proof of neutering is produced. Don't be a careless Chessie breeder.

Registering and Showing Your Chesapeake

The American Kennel Club

The American Kennel Club (AKC) has registered at least one million dogs each year since 1970; in 1996, 1,332,557 purebred dogs were registered. It is the largest U.S. kennel club. Founded in 1884, the AKC is a nonprofit organization dedicated to the welfare and advancement of purebred dogs.

The AKC does not license kennels or individual dog breeders, but does train and license dog show judges. It adopts and enforces rules and regulations governing dog shows and other purebred canine exhibitions. The events that are held under AKC rules include conformation dog shows, obedience trials, agility contests, tracking trials, field trials, hunting tests, and herding tests and trials.

The registry maintains the standards of all breeds recognized by the club, and currently registers 143 breeds that are separated into seven groups for the purpose of exhibition. Those groups include Sporting (including Chesapeake), Hound, Working, Terrier, Toy, Non-sporting, and Herding.

Perhaps this organization's greatest contribution to dogdom is the information they provide to anyone who is interested in promoting dog ownership and stewardship. Although there are other U.S. dog registries, the AKC is far and away the most influential.

Litter Registration

Data from various AKC documents are used for the following discussion. Other registries' policies and rules may vary, but the principles are the same.

When a litter is born, the owners of both the sire and dam complete and sign a Litter Registration Application form that is sent to the registry accompanied by an appropriate fee. When the application is received, AKC mails a "litter kit" to the dam's owner. It includes a blue-colored, partially completed registration application form for each puppy. One of those blue slips should accompany each puppy when it is sold.

The blue form lists the AKC litter registration number, sire and dam's registration numbers, breeder information, and sex of the pup. The breeder completes the form to show the puppy's color and markings, date purchased, and buyer's name and address.

The puppy may also be named on the blue slip, but be forewarned that once a dog's name is registered it can't be changed. The AKC invites complex names to better identify each dog. Simple names like Rusty or Fido just won't do! This form should be signed by the buyer and sent to the AKC with a fee.

After the blue slip is completed and mailed to the registry with a fee, a permanent *AKC Registration Certificate* is printed and mailed to the new owner. Co-ownership or limited registration of purebred dogs is also possible.

Pedigrees

A pedigree is a genealogical document; it is a family tree. It is of great value, almost indispensable, if the dog is bred. It may contain three or four generations of a registered dog's ancestry. Breeders often prepare pedigrees on blank forms, or on computer formats. These are not official documents, but if accurate, they furnish the same information as an AKC pedigree.

If an official AKC pedigree is desired, it can be purchased from the registry for a fee. These documents list AKC exhibition titles as well as the names and registration numbers of three or four generations of the dog's ancestors. An indication of the dog's hip conformation as determined by the OFA may be included as well.

Conformation Shows

Those dog owners whose interests lie in other directions sometimes call conformation competition or dog shows "beauty pageants." That term isn't really fair and doesn't quite cover the subject. Conformation shows are designed to promote superior quality registered, purebred dogs and to identify breeding stock or potential breeding stock. In order to be eligible for showing, a dog must be intact; that is, not spayed or neutered. It must be free of hereditary diseases and deformities to the best of the judges' knowledge. In order to win in a show, the exhibited dog must be of the correct size and color. It must have the correct type and amount of coat, and move with a sound and balanced gait.

The ideal Chessie is one that matches the breed standard that is written by Chessie clubs and adopted by the AKC. Dog shows are designed

A show dog with a sporting background.

to judge dogs of the same breed and sex against one another, and points are awarded for specific class wins, depending upon the number of competitors entered.

Titles

A number of titles are assigned to winners of competitive events that are authorized by the AKC. That organization currently regulates and furnishes judges for seven events. Of those, Chessies may compete in five (see Work for Your Chesapeake, beginning on page 62). The remaining event for which registered Chessies are eligible is conformation showing. That endeavor is treated separately because it represents a different but important phase of Chesapeake ownership.

Although having a dog that wins a prestigious title is a rewarding experience for the Chessie owner, a feeling of accomplishment will come with each near miss as well. Each time Rowdy competes, you learn something of the Chessie, and he learns from you. To own a dog that drives boldly across

Entering your Chessie in competition can be fun for both of you.

A show dog must be clean and well groomed, but the Chessie requires no special coat trimming to be shown. Nails, of course, should be trimmed neatly. Show dogs must be manageable and trustworthy, because control is a vital part of participation in shows.

Before making a decision to begin a show career for your pup, consult with Chessie breeders in your local club. Have Rowdy "faulted" or judged by someone who has been involved with the breed for a while and has shown dogs. If the pup isn't mature enough, or has an obvious problem, this experienced person should be able to point it out to you.

If it appears that Rowdy has the quality to win, enroll him in classes. Many specialty clubs and all-breed dog clubs have regular conformation classes for novice dogs. Enter Rowdy in fun matches for experience (yours and his). If all goes well in the classes and matches, you are ready for the big time. If you decide to enter him in a dog show, you may elect to exhibit him yourself or hire a professional handler.

A show dog and his handler must work as a team. Rowdy must obey his handler instantly, and he must look to the handler for direction. He can't be easily distracted, and must stand very still when the judge runs his hands over him. Rowdy can't resent being lifted a tiny bit by the tail, or having his scrotum handled when the judge checks to see that he has normal testicles. The judge may also open Rowdy's lips to expose his bite. The dog must accept these invasions of privacy with good nature, and a little tail wagging doesn't hurt his chances a bit.

the ring and receives the applause of the bystanders gives you a feeling of pride. To show well is an accomplishment in itself, for the dog and handler. To win is the ultimate thrill!

The title awarded to an animal that has proved its merit by earning sufficient points according to AKC rules is Champion of Record. That title is abbreviated Ch. and is added as a prefix to a dog's AKC-registered name. A Champion of Record is a dog that has accumulated at least fifteen points that have been awarded by at least three different judges. The points awarded vary according to the number of dogs of the same breed that are entered, and cannot exceed five at any show. Only two dogs at each show earn points. The total points leading to championship must include two wins of no less than three points each (major wins). To earn a Ch. is not as easy as it may sound!

Show Dogs

All registered Chesapeakes can be entered in a show providing they have reached the minimal age of six months, are physically normal, and have been trained sufficiently to behave in the ring.

Handlers

An owner who wishes to be a handler shouldn't try to exhibit a dog without the benefit of some classes and instruction. Breed and all-breed clubs usually hold handler classes at least once a year. If a child has aspirations of handling the family dog in an AKC show, start the youngster's junior handling education early. Although no preference is given to children handlers, a well-dressed child handling a fine Chesapeake will quickly get the attention of the audience and judge.

A prospective handler should attend dog shows to see what is expected. When the judge tells the handler "up and back," the reaction should be instantaneous. Sometimes judges call their top dogs out of competition very quietly, and the handler must listen carefully. Nothing is more embarrassing than having your dog chosen and not realizing it until the judge shouts "*Chesapeake,*" to the gallery's amusement.

Entries

The AKC is particular about entries. Everything must be in order on the dog's registration, and the application must be correctly filed and mailed by a deadline date. Your dog will compete against other Chessies of the same sex.

Breed Standard

The Official Standard for the Chessie can be obtained from your Chessie club or from the AKC. Highlights from that standard are given here.

The Chesapeake's head is broad with a medium muzzle with small ears and eyes of yellowish or amber color. The chest should be deep and wide and show strength. The body should be of medium length with the flanks well tucked up.

The hindquarters are high and show considerable power for swimming, and the back should be short and powerful. The stifles are well angulated. Legs are all straight with good bone and muscle. The toes are webbed and the dog has no hind dewclaws.

The tail is straight or only slightly curved, extends to the hock, and is moderately feathered. It does not curl over the dog's back.

The Chesapeake's coat is thick and short with a dense fine wooly undercoat. The facial and leg hair is short and straight and tends to be wavy on the shoulders, neck, back, and loins only. Curly coat is not permissible. Coat texture and color are two of the most important features of the Chesapeake. It is important that the coat is resistant to water, oily and thick to protect the dog from extreme weather conditions. It is self-colored to blend with his surroundings when duck hunting, and is dead grass in varying degrees from tan to dull straw color. Small white spots are permissible on the breast, toes, and belly.

Males range from 65 to 80 pounds (29–36 kg) and stand from 23 to 26 inches (58–66 cm), and females from 55 to 70 pounds (25–32 kg) and stand from 21 to 24 inches (53–61 cm). Oversized or undersized dogs are penalized.

The Chesapeake is a bright and happy dog with an intelligent expression. It is well proportioned, has a good coat, and is well balanced. It must have courage, willingness to work, alertness, nose, intelligence, a love of water, and a good disposition.

The specific disqualifications include black color, dewclaws on hind legs, white on any part of the body except those mentioned, and feathering on tail or legs in excess of 1.75 inches (4.4 cm) in length. An undershot or overshot jaw and an overall curly coat also are disqualifying features.

The breed standard lists a scale of points to be used when judging, and a table of approximate measurements for every anatomical dimension of the

Winning Best in Group is quite an honor.

body. The Chesapeake standard also contains a note, which states that "the question of coat and general type of balance takes precedence over any scoring table which could be drawn up."

Judging

AKC judges mentally compare each dog in the class with the "perfect" Chessie as described by the standard. Allowances are made for age, maturity, and differences between the sexes. The judge must be conversant with virtually every point in the breed standard and make placements accordingly. Conforma-

tion dogs are not judged on the basis of the breed standard alone. Judges have the responsibility to consider the dog's attitude and conditioning. Training and willingness are important parts of showing, and a dog that is enjoying itself has a better chance at winning than one that is just going through the motions.

Types of Shows

There are two types of dog shows: specialty and all-breed events. Specialty shows are limited to dogs of a particular breed or group of similar breeds. All-breed shows are unlimited and all registered dogs may be entered. Individual dog clubs manage the shows that are held under AKC rules. Every recognized breed has a national parent club as well as local specialty clubs.

The parent club has the responsibility of revising and clarifying the official standards of their breed, and after the parent club has approved changes, they can be submitted to the AKC for its final approval.

Classes

There are five classes in which a dog may compete for points toward its championship. The puppy class is often divided into two groups: six to nine months and nine to twelve months. The novice class, bred-by-exhibitor class, American-bred class, and open class are the others in which dogs may compete.

Judging of every breed follows the same routine, and the males compete only with other males, and bitches are judged against other bitches. The reason for which a dog was bred has no bearing on how it is judged in a conformation show.

First, the puppy dogs (males) are judged, with four placements awarded to each class with the first place remaining in competition.

The Novice dogs, Bred-by-Exhibitor, American-bred, and Open dog classes (males) are judged individually and the first-place dogs from each class are brought back into the ring to compete again. This judging of first-place winners is called the Winners Class, and the winner of this class is called the Winners Dog. That dog receives championship points at the show. The dog that placed second to the Winners Dog in its original class is brought into the ring to compete with the other class winners for Reserve Winners Dog. If the Winners Dog is disqualified by the AKC for any

Good style and concentration on the retrieve.

reason, the Reserve Winners Dog receives the points.

Then the process is repeated for the bitches to find the Winners Bitch (the only bitch to receive points at the show) and Reserve Winners Bitch.

The next class to be judged is made up of all entered Champions of Record (male and female), the Winners Dog, and the Winners Bitch. This is called the Best of Breed class, and from it is selected the single animal that the judge considers the Best of Breed in the show. Then the judge selects the Best of Winners from the Winners Dog and Winners Bitch. If one of those two dogs has already been selected as Best of Breed, that animal is automatically the Best of Winners. Finally, a Best of Opposite Sex is chosen from the class.

In a specialty show, that concludes the judging. In an all-breed show, the Best of Breed winner competes in its group, for placement in the group. The dogs chosen as best in each of the seven groups compete for Best in Show.

Whether or not your Chessie earns AKC championship status, he will always be a champion in your heart.

In dual-purpose dogs (dogs that are trained for field as well as conformation showing) the ultimate title of dual champion is awarded to dogs that have earned their Champion of Record title in conformation shows, as well as a Field Champion title in field (retriever) trials. It designates a dog of superior conformation in which few faults were found; it is a talented hunter that has been judged against other field dogs and hasn't come away wanting.

A Triple Champion is a dog that has earned a Field Champion title, a Champion of Record title, and an Obedience Trial Champion title. Such a dog, I think, would be the absolute paragon to possess. For the average Chessie owner, however, perhaps that goal is a bit high; it requires a near perfect dog and thousands of hours of training to accomplish.

If you began with an outstanding puppy and are dedicated and as willing to work as your Chessie is, that lofty goal is achievable. If however, Rowdy's role in your family is that of an obedient, lovable, loyal friend that is always ready for a romp, swim, or a bit of serious retrieving, he can bring you nearly as much joy as winning in competition. Unfortunately, there are no certificates to hang on the wall, no titles or rosettes awarded to the best companion on the block, and only you will know that Rowdy is a true champion at heart.

Useful Addresses and Literature

Clubs

Amateur Field Trial Clubs of America
360 Winchester Lane
Stanton, TN 38069

American Chesapeake Club
Audrey Austin
18331 Highway 94
Dulzura, CA 91917

Canadian Chesapeake Club
192 King Street W.
P.O. Box 217
Woodville, Ontario Canada KOM 2TO

Hunting Retriever Club
Rt. 1, Box 132
Simsboro, LA 71275

National Retriever Club of Canada
1348 Mills Road RR2
Sydney, BC Canada V8L 3S1

National Shoot to Retrieve Association
226 North Mill Street #2
Plainfield, IN 46168

North American Versatile Hunting Dog
  Association
Box 529
Arlington Heights, IL 60006

Associations

American Boarding Kennel Association
4575 Galley Road, Suite 400-A
Colorado Springs, CO 80915

American Humane Association
9725 E. Hampton Avenue
Denver, CO 80231

American Kennel Club
51 Madison Avenue
New York, NY 10010
Web site: http://www.AKC.org

For Registration, Records, Litter
  Information:
5580 Centerview Drive
Raleigh, NC 27606

American Veterinary Medical
  Association
930 No. Meacham Road
Schaumburg, IL 60173

Canadian Kennel Club
111 Eglington Avenue
Toronto 12, Ontario
Canada

Canine Eye Registry Foundation
  (CERF)
South Campus Court, Building C
West Lafayette, IN 47907

Institute for Genetic Disease Control
  (GDC)
P.O. Box 222
Davis, CA 95617

Kennel Club, The
1–4 Clargis Street
Picadilly London W7Y8AB
England

Morris Animal Foundation
45 Inverness Drive E.
Englewood, CO 80112-5480

A fine dog with an American heritage.

American Field, The
542 South Dearborn Street
Chicago, IL 60605

Dog Fancy Magazine
P.O. Box 53264
Boulder, CO 80322-3264

Dog World
29 North Wacker Drive
Chicago, IL 60606

Gaines Touring With Towser
P.O. Box 5700
Kankakee, IL 60902

Gun Dog
Stover Publications Company
P.O. Box 35098
Des Moines, IA 50315

Hunting Retriever
United Kennel Club
100 E. Kilgore Road
Kalamazoo, MI 49001-5598

National Dog Registry (tattoo, microchip)
P.O. Box 116
Woodstock, NY 12498

Orthopedic Foundation for Animals
(OFA)
2300 Nifong Boulevard
Columbia, MO 65201

Owner Handler Association of
America
583 Knoll Court
Seaford, NY 11783

Tattoo-A-Pet
Dept. 1625
Emmons Avenue
Brooklyn, NY 11235

Periodicals
AKC Gazette
51 Madison Avenue
New York, NY 10010

Books
Alderton, David. *Dogs.* New York: DK
    Publishing Company, 1993.
American Kennel Club. *The Complete
    Dog Book.* New York: Macmillan
    Publishing Co., 1992.
Breed Book of The Newfoundland
    Club of America. *This Is the New-
    foundland.* New York: TFH Publica-
    tions, Inc., 1978.
Bulanda, Susan. *The Canine Source
    Book.* Wilsonvile, OR:
    Doral Publishing Inc., 1990.
Chern, Margaret B. *The Complete
    Newfoundland.* New York: Howell
    Book House, Inc., 1987.
Cherry, Eloise H. *The Complete
    Chesapeake Bay Retriever.* New
    York: Howell Book House, Inc., 1983.
Clark, Ross D. and Stainer, Joan R.
    *Medical & Genetic Aspects of
    Purebred Dogs.* Fairway, KS and
    St. Simons Island, GA: Forum
    Publications, Inc., 1994.

Every Chessie is a champion at heart.

Davis, Henry P. *Modern Dog Encyclopedia*. Harrisburg, PA: The Stackpole Company, 1958.

Fogel, Bruce. *First Aid For Dogs*. New York: Penguin Books, 1997.

Free, James L. *Training Your Retriever*. New York: Coward, McCann & Geoghegan, Inc., 1977.

Heller, Eloise C. *The Complete Chesapeake Bay Retriever*. New York: Howell Book House, Inc., 1983.

Holland, Ray P. *Bird Dogs*. New York: A.S. Barnes & Company, 1948.

Horn, Janet. *The New Complete Chesapeake Bay Retriever*. New York: Howell Book House, Inc., 1994.

Lorenz, Michael D. and Cornelius, Larry M. *Small Animal Medical Diagnosis*. Philadelphia: J.B. Lippincott Company, 1993.

Michener, James A. *Chesapeake*. New York: Fawcett Crest, 1978.

Myrus, Don. *Dog Catalog*. New York: Macmillan Publishing Co., 1978.

Rice, Dan F. *The Complete Book of Dog Breeding*. New York: Barron's Educational Series, Inc., 1997.

Rowan, A. Hamilton, Chairman of Production. *AKC's World of the Purebred Dog*. New York: Howell Book House, Inc., 1983.

Waters, B. *Fetch and Carry*. Printed in 1895 by B. Waters.

Wolters, Richard A. *Duck Dogs*. New York: E. P. Dutton, 1990.

———. *Water Dog*. New York: E. P. Dutton, 1964.

Yamazaki, Tetsu. *Legacy of the Dog*. San Francisco: Chronicle Books, 1995.

Index

Age considerations, 24–25
Agility trials, 70–71
Aging, 87–88
American:
  Association of Feed Control
    Officials (AAFCO), 51, 53
  Chesapeake Club (ACC), 12–13,
    17, 28, 99
  Kennel Club (AKC), 30, 92, 99
Appetite, 75
Automobiles, travel, 37–38

Bathing, 59
Bloat, 80–81
Boarding kennels, 38
Bonding, 31–32
Bordetella, 79
Breed:
  history, 9–13
  qualities, 14–20
  standard, 95–96
Breeders, 28–30
Breeding, 89–91
  pedigree examination, 90–91
  puppies, finding homes, 91
  stock selection, 90

Calluses, 60
Canine:
  distemper, 78
  Good Citizen Award, 62, 71
  hip dysplasia, 86–87
Canned food, 50–51
Car:
  accidents, 75
  travel, 37–38
Carbohydrates, 54
Chesapeake Bay, 8–9
Chesapeake Bay Retriever types,
  25, 28
Chewing, 37
Choke collar, 43–44
Coat, 14–15
  color, 15, 27
  quality, 54–55
Collar:
  choke, 43–44
  pronged, 44

training, 42–43
Combing, 58
"Come" command, 44–46
Commands, 44–49
Commercial food brands,
  51–52
Companion dogs, 28
Competition, 17
  agility trials, 70–71
  Canine Good Citizen, 71
  conformation shows, 93–98
  hunting tests, 67
  obedience trials, 67–69
  retriever field trials, 66–67
  tracking dog, 69–70
Conformation shows, 93–98
Coronavirus, 78–79
Cost considerations, 21
Crate training, 33–34
Cryptorchidism, 85

Dental care, 60–61
Dewclaws, 27
Diet, 31, 50–56
  carbohydrates, 54
  fats, 53–54
  feeding frequency, 55
  homemade, 55
  obesity, 55–56
  protein, 53
  vitamins, 50
    supplements, 54
  water, 53
Diseases, 78–81
  aging, 87–88
Distemper, 78
Domestication, 6–8
"Down" command, 47
Dry foods, 51–52
Dual-purpose dogs, 17
Dummies, 63–64

Ear care, 59
Emergencies, 74–77
Entropion, 87
Epilepsy, 86
Euthanasia, 88
Exercise, 36–37

Eyes:
  care, 59
  inspecting, 27

Family dog, 18–19
Fats, 53–54
Feeding, 50–56
  carbohydrates, 54
  diet "no-no's," 55
  fats, 53–54
  frequency, 55
  obesity, 55–56
  protein, 53
  trials, 52–53
  vitamin supplements, 54
  water, 53
Field trials, 17, 25, 67
Fleas, 83–84
Food, 50–55
  homemade diets, 55
  labels, 52–53
  types, 50–52
Footpad lacerations, 77

Gastric torsion, 80–81
Gender considerations, 23–24, 27
Grooming, 57–61
  bathing, 59
  calluses, 60
  combing, 58
  dental care, 60–61
  ear care, 59
  equipment, 58
  eye care, 59
  nail care, 58–59
Gundogs, 25, 62–63
Guns, 64–65
Gunshot, 77

Handlers, 94–95
Hazards, 34–35
Health:
  care, 73–88
  considerations, 23
  inspection, 26–27
  preventative medicine, 78–81
  records, 30
Heart rate, 75